DAVID J. SCHMIDT

Three Nights in the Clown Motel

Written and illustrated by
David J. Schmidt

DAVID J. SCHMIDT

Copyright © 2017 David J. Schmidt
All rights reserved. First edition.

All photos and illustrations are by David J. Schmidt.

ISBN-13: 978-1976182587
ISBN-10: 1976182581

DISCLAIMER

This book does not represent the viewpoints of the Clown Motel or its owners or employees.

To protect the privacy of the individuals involved, many of their names have been changed. Many of the conversations quoted herein have been paraphrased, as they were not recorded. Nonetheless, all the events described in this book actually happened. This is no horror movie—this is real.

THREE NIGHTS IN THE CLOWN MOTEL

Dedicated to my brother, who is even more afraid of clowns than I am.

DAVID J. SCHMIDT

THREE NIGHTS IN THE CLOWN MOTEL

"Want your boat, Georgie?" Pennywise asked. "I only repeat myself because you really do not seem that eager." He held it up, smiling. He was wearing a baggy silk suit with great big orange buttons. A bright tie, electric-blue, flopped down his front, and on his hands were big white gloves [...]
"Yes, sure," George said, looking into the storm drain.
"And a balloon? I've got red and green and yellow and blue..."
"Do they float?"
"Float?" The clown's grin widened. "Oh yes, indeed they do. They float! And there's cotton candy..."
George reached.
The clown seized his arm.
And George saw the clown's face change.
    -*IT,* Stephen King

DAVID J. SCHMIDT

THREE NIGHTS IN THE CLOWN MOTEL

Table of Contents

CHAPTER		**PAGE**
	Introduction	11
1	Leaving Home	18
2	Desert Accent	24
3	"Free Coffee"	27
4	The Gods of Fear	32
5	Death Valley	36
6	The Motel	40
7	An Infestation of Clowns	46
8	Voices in the Graveyard	51
9	Paint on His Face and Spikes on His Teeth	58
10	Twisted Faces	63
11	Mass Graves	67
12	Mister Creepy	71
13	The Hissing	75
14	The Moving Hand	80
15	"Don't Tempt Fate"	85
16	"They Are Still Here"	91
17	"It Followed Her Home"	95
18	Solitude	100
19	Dread	105
20	Cemetery	109
21	"Something Is Here"	116
22	The Clowns I Fear	121
23	A Lovely Day in Death Valley	127

DAVID J. SCHMIDT

Introduction

"Clowns have always been associated with danger and fear, because they push logic up to its breaking point. They push our understanding to the limits of reason and they do this through joking but also through ridicule."

    -Andrew Stott, British professor and specialist in clown culture

The face behind the tombstone

One of my earliest childhood memories involves clowns.

My parents took me to Disneyland when I was five, and they happened to have a circus-themed event that summer. Clowns were everywhere.

Faces pale, lips blood red. Grimacing, cackling, lurching back and forth on stilts, bending down to glare at me. Baring their teeth like apes do before they attack. Even the other children my age had their faces painted—hundreds of clowns walking past me at eye level.

After an hour, I'd had enough. I asked my parents to take me on a ride. The nearest one was the Haunted Mansion.

It was fun and relaxing, at first. Paintings that stretched on their own; silly songs playing in minor key; cool air conditioning. Zero clowns. Our circular cart slid down the track between gnarled trees, cracked tombstones, and cawing crows. Animatronic creatures danced and sang the upbeat song, *Grim Grinning Ghosts.*

The cart suddenly swiveled to face a row of tombstones. One of them was much bigger than the others—an exaggerated, carved form swelled wide at the top. Something behind it caught my eye:

a shimmering white form. I leaned over the lap bar to get a closer look.

It jumped out.

A hideous face glowed phosphorescent in the dark, gaping black holes where its eyes should have been, its mouth in a wide clown-like grimace. I screamed.

Ever since that day, the two images were fused in my mind: the painted faces and the corpse leaping from its casket. The wide red smiles and the empty eye sockets of a skull.

The clowns and the graveyard.

Clowns: What are we so afraid of?

A psychologist friend recently told me about a patient who suffers from a crippling case of *coulrophobia,* the fear of clowns. The patient couldn't even say the word "clown" when she first came to my friend's office. Only after months of intensive therapy could she stand to look at a photograph of one.

While my coulrophobia isn't that bad, the fear of clowns definitely runs in my family.

When my father was five years old, he dreamed that he met a clown at the local gas station. The clown smiled at him with teeth covered in long metal spikes. Most of my cousins on both sides of the family are frightened by clowns. My brother is terrified of them. I called him up recently to ask him why.

"What's *not* creepy about clowns?" he scoffed. "They're just 'off' enough to be unsettling. A clown looks humanoid, but it's all distorted: huge hands and feet, wild, unnaturally colored hair. It talks in a weird, high voice, with way too much inappropriate, forced laughter. A clown is a walking bundle of cognitive dissonance—it's kind of human, but not fully human.

"Not to mention, you can't see its face. The heavy makeup makes it impossible to accurately read its emotions."

When I asked my uncle Craig the same question, his answer was more succinct: "Why am I scared of them? Because clowns are fucking creepy."

My family is not alone. Researchers estimate that between seven and twelve percent of the U.S. population suffer from coulrophobia. In a *Vox* poll of nearly 2,000 readers, 42% of respondents said they fear clowns. When the University of Sheffield was planning a new children's hospital, they asked 250 British children what decorations they preferred. Not a single child liked clowns.

Sigmund Freud described our fear of the uncanny as *"das Unheimliche,"* something that is both familiar and frightening at the same time. As my brother observed, clowns can look like a cruel parody of the human form.

Maybe we are frightened by the clown's anonymity, the human evil that hides behind the mask. The character of the "masked trickster" goes all the way back to the Norse cult of Loki and the native cultures of the Pacific Northwest. In the modern mythology of the slasher film, some of the most well-known killers wear masks: Jason, Leatherface, Michael Myers. With their true identity obscured, their dark impulses are set loose.

In 1986—the same year I saw the clowns at Disneyland—the world was introduced to a new face of terror: Pennywise the Dancing Clown. Stephen King's novel *IT*, and the 1990 television miniseries based on it, made an entire generation of children afraid to walk over storm drains. (Including yours truly.) The "creepy clown" figure is now a mainstay of horror movies, from *Killer Clowns from Outer Space* to a host of B-movies, to the blockbuster remake of *IT* this year.

Sometimes the horror bleeds over from fantasy into reality. Fans of the horror-core band *Insane Clown Posse,* known as "Juggalos," have been involved in a series of violent crimes, often while dressed as clowns. In 2011, two *I.C.P.* fans, Shawn Freemore and Ian Seagraves, were convicted in a Pennsylvania court of murdering Michael Goucher with a hatchet. Their fellow Juggalos posted clown photos and messages online expressing support for the murder.

The most famous killer clown of recent history is John Wayne Gacy. Between 1972 and 1978, he raped, tortured, and murdered at least 33 people. He wasn't the first, though.

Jean-Gaspard Deburau was one of Europe's most famous clowns of the 19th century. He was so well-known that people recognized him in public, even without his white face paint and bright red lips. One day in 1836, a young boy insulted Deburau on the streets of Paris. The clown killed the boy with a blow from his walking stick.

Associating clowns with the tragic and macabre is nothing new, either. In *The Pickwick Papers,* Charles Dickens describes a clown character in grotesque, despondent terms. The title character of the 1892 opera *Pagliacci* is a clown who murders his wife in full costume. In 1876, French literary critic Edmond de Goncourt said a clown's performance can be "terrifying, full of anxiety and apprehension." In recent years, however, the "creepy clown" trope has exploded into a true epidemic.

Witnesses have spotted them in Europe, Asia, Latin America, and Australia. In the shadows, on street corners, under bridges. The clowns are everywhere.

In 2014, European newspapers reported an outbreak of "clown-related violence" in France. In Chile, a teen filmed a clown who chased after him with a baseball bat. Two twelve-year-old Australian girls were buying ice cream with their father when a clown attacked them and tried to steal their phone. Ten clowns in Finland chased a group of children under a bridge, where another clown waited with a chainsaw. A clown with an axe broke into a young woman's home in Ireland and terrorized her. The country with the most clown-sightings by far, however, is the United States.

In the summer of 2016, a group of children in South Carolina came across several clowns lurking in the woods. The clowns invited them to "come visit their cabin in the forest." On September 29 of the same year, an Ohio woman was smoking on her front porch when a clown ran up and grabbed her by the neck. "I should just kill you now," he said. Two days later, a Kentucky woman was walking down a wooded trail at night when a clown jumped out of the trees, assaulted her, and attempted to drag her off into the forest.

Hundreds of other witnesses have seen them. While some clowns get violent, however, most of them don't *do* anything—they just stand there. By the roadside, in the forest, on a dark city street. Staring. Waiting.

Their inscrutability might be the scariest thing about these clowns. Who are they? What do they want? Why do they do it?

At the height of these clown sightings, I had the bright idea to drive into the desert and visit the Clown Motel.

The Motel

It started with a text message from my cousin Melanie, who knows how much I love the sinister and the macabre. Melanie is always there to support my next ghost-hunting project.

"Hey, David, have you heard of this place?" she sent me a link to a news article. "Apparently, there is a haunted clown motel somewhere in the desert of Nevada."

My curiosity was piqued. I did some research.

A quick Google search of the words "clown motel nevada" produced these headlines:

- *AMERICA'S SCARIEST MOTEL*

- *MOTEL HAUNTED BY HUNDREDS OF CLOWNS*
- *THIS CREEPY CLOWN MOTEL IN NEVADA IS THE STUFF NIGHTMARES ARE MADE OF*

Articles and reviews of the place followed the same tone:

- *It smells like people might have died in there. Not my type of place...*
- *Spending the night in the Clown Motel qualifies as a true test of courage...*
- *This not-so-amusing inn is no place for the timid...*

I learned that the Clown Motel—its official name—stands on the outskirts of the small town of Tonopah, Nevada, population 2,478. In technical terms, Tonopah is located at the crossroads of U.S. highways 6 and 95, halfway between Reno and Las Vegas. In layman's terms, it is located in the middle of freaking nowhere. It looked to be just an eight hour drive from San Diego, though—very doable.

I found some photos of the place online. The neon sign announced *CLOWN MOTEL* in red block letters, surrounded by twinkling lights. Above the motel's name, a clown wearing a pointed hat, with red lips and a matching nose, juggled three balls in the air. His eyes were half-shut, a vague look of Zen contentment on his face. The motel was little more than a weather-worn building in the middle of the desert. The lobby was filled with hundreds of clown dolls. Definitely a creepy place.

Not to mention, it was located next door to a cemetery.

And not just any cemetery—this was a genuine, Old West boot hill, full of the rotting remains of gunslingers and prostitutes. Not surprisingly, people said the place was haunted as hell.

The television show *"Ghost Adventures"* filmed an episode there. A Fox News anchor interviewed a guest who claimed to have seen the silhouette of a clown staring in his window at night.

As someone who writes about haunted places for a living, the Clown Motel was a must-see. Anyone can spend the night on the Queen Mary, or visit the haunted Whaley House. But a Clown Motel in the middle of the desert, next to a graveyard? The experience would be one-of-a-kind.

I had an ulterior motive in going there as well, however: I had something to prove to myself. The clowns, the graveyard—it was like a nightmare dredged up from early childhood. This would be my chance to finally face those old demons head-on. A showdown in the desert.

This wasn't just business. This was personal.

So it was that I left San Diego one cold March morning in 2017, and embarked on a journey to the edge of civilization, to the ghost towns of Nevada's mining country, in search of the truth behind the mysterious Clown Motel. The fact that I chose to do so at the height of a worldwide clown epidemic did not fully dawn on me until I was already far from home.

In retrospect, it might have been bad timing.

CHAPTER 1
Leaving Home

To me, clowns aren't funny. In fact, they're kind of scary. I've wondered where this started and I think it goes back to the time I went to the circus, and a clown killed my dad.
    -*Deep Thoughts* by comedian Jack Handy

When I first planned the trip, I tried to get a friend or two to come along.

"What are you doing this weekend?" I asked my buddy Kirk.

"Going to a Slipknot concert. Why?"

"I'm driving out to a haunted Clown Motel."

"AND HE WAS NEVER HEARD FROM AGAIN," Kirk said melodramatically. I replied with a nervous laugh.

The next four people I contacted also had plans that weekend. The fifth friend simply texted back: *CLOWN Motel? Not in a million years.*

It looked like I would be going alone.

I called up the motel to reserve a room for three nights.

"Do you have a preference of upstairs or downstairs?" I was surprised by how normal the receptionist's voice sounded. I half-expected her to speak with a clown-like falsetto.

"Uh... I'll take upstairs." I figured that would put me at least marginally farther away from any psycho who might show up with a hatchet.

"Smoking or non-smoking?" The receptionist asked.

"Non-smoking, please." I immediately considered changing it to smoking. I was already stressed out about spending the weekend in this place, and wondered if some secondhand nicotine might be calming.

The woman asked me for a credit card to reserve the room.

"Is it all right if I just pay in cash?"

"Well, we need to take down a credit card number... You can just make up a number, though. I just need to put something on this form for my boss."

"Um, okay...the card is number 1234-5678..."

"Go on..."

"And the last eight digits...8765-4321."

"Very good, sir."

While I was glad that nobody would steal my credit card information over the phone, I was concerned by the motel's lax security standards. If they didn't check my ID, they didn't do it for any of the other guests, either. Whatever mysterious characters stayed at the Clown Motel, I would be sleeping next door to them in the middle of the desert.

* * * *

My plan was to leave San Diego at 9:00 a.m., giving me plenty of time to drive across the desert. I was hesitant, dragging my feet, checking my phone over and over, packing and repacking the same t-shirt three times. A nebulous sense of apprehension at the back of my mind caused me to procrastinate. Finally, by noon, I was ready to go.

In addition to a couple changes of clothes, I packed my laptop, phone charger, and Stephen King's *IT*. I considered bringing my shotgun. The news stories about clown sightings were on my mind—ghosts, I could handle, but what if some nut showed up outside my window in a clown costume? I didn't know the laws for taking weapons across state lines, however, so I settled for a nice baseball bat.

I checked my car's oil levels before hitting the road. When I lifted the hood, a crow flapped right past my face, startling me with a loud *PAP PAP PAP PAP*. If my life were a scary movie, this would be the first cheap jump scare in the film—the one that sets the scene and makes viewers shout, "It's a sign! Get out while you can!"

* * * *

The 15 freeway took me north, between rolling hills and avocado groves, lush and green from the recent rain. I passed through the suburban centers of Escondido and Temecula, where tract homes and chain restaurants lined the freeway.

The news anchors on the radio discussed a recent surge of suicides in the San Diego area. A jumper had stood on the busiest freeway overpass in town, at the junction of the 5, 163, and 8 freeways, holding up traffic for hours. At roughly the same time, a woman in Oceanside stepped in front of an Amtrak train. Two hours later, a woman parked her car on the San Diego-Coronado Bridge and jumped to her death. Just minutes later, a man parked his car on the shoulder of Interstate 8 and shot himself.

The news then reported on a high school shooting. It wasn't the first one that month.

If my life were a horror movie, I thought, *this would be more foreshadowing, telling you that some cataclysmic disaster or zombie apocalypse lies just around the corner.*

After I passed suburban Temecula, the freeway forked off into the 215 and headed east. The landscape changed notably at this point. Manicured trees and parks gave way to pure concrete, punctuated by empty dirt lots. Applebee's turned into Del Taco; country clubs turned into gun clubs; the smiling real estate agents on the billboards turned into strippers.

There is an invisible line that you cross somewhere around this point, much more significant than the political separation between California and Nevada: it is the line that divides urban California from The Desert.

The freeway took a sharp turn uphill and snaked through a range of mountains. Signs of life became much more sparse in the tawny, sun-baked hills. Eighteen-wheelers crawled up the cracked asphalt. A lone crow followed me overhead for several miles.

Another hour passed before I came to the next human settlement. The town of Adelanto is little more than a small strip mall of franchises at the crossroads—a Starbucks, Rite Aid, and a Rubio's Fish Taco—in an otherwise desolate setting. Most of Adelanto consists of trailers, boarded up buildings, and what feels like hundreds of churches. Its people walk around slowly, slouched under the hot sun, the only shade coming from their own brows.

John Steinbeck wrote, in *Travels with Charley in Search of America*, one of the best descriptions of desert dwellers I have ever seen:

> *There is a breed of desert men, not hiding exactly but gone to sanctuary [...] These men have not changed with the exploding times except to die and be replaced by others like them.*

The people who manage to survive this far from cities and water and grass are a unique breed indeed. One part of me feels like they would have the best chances of surviving a nuclear holocaust. Another part feels like they already have.

Several miles after passing Adelanto, I saw a weathered woman standing next to a stroller. I couldn't tell if the bundle in it was a human child or a pile of her belongings. Not thumbing a ride, not trying to cross the road—just standing and staring into the distance. Her presence was an absolute mystery. The only witnesses to her silent struggle were the jagged Joshua trees with their wild arms akimbo, the tumbleweeds, and the baked earth of the vast, eternal desert. And yet, the woman somehow survived out there.

My mind wandered to some of the videos of "clown sightings" I had watched before leaving San Diego. In many of them, the clowns appear in rural areas, miles from the nearest town.

What possesses a person to do that? I wondered. *What makes a person put on a clown outfit and go stand in the middle of nowhere? Is it just to get a reaction out of people? Is this some antisocial instinct that possesses certain people? Is it the first sign of a total breakdown of society?*

Not long ago, a friend told me that her brother was one of these clowns. He and his comrades frequently put on their costumes and drove out to abandoned buildings. I looked him up on Facebook. In the chilling photos, the young men hold pistols and semiautomatic weapons, staring menacingly into the camera. I asked my friend why they do it—why put so much effort into this antisocial display of aggression? Her reply was succinct: "My brother... He's not well."

Something suddenly caught my eye. A flash of color by the roadside. A clown. Up ahead, at the next curve in the road. He stood at the edge of the desert, dressed in a bright orange costume.

I blinked and took a second look. It was a construction worker wearing a fluorescent orange vest. He stood waving the traffic over into the right lane, before a line of cones that blocked off half the road. I slowed to 5 MPH and merged with the rest of the cars.

The traffic cones must have been part of my confusion, I thought. *With the sun in my eyes, they could have looked like pointy clown hats. I'm safe, though; It's just a construction crew. No antisocial, killer clowns out here...*

At that instant, a pickup truck whizzed past on my left. Beneath the *TRUMP 2016* sticker on his back window, a larger one announced: *I DO WHAT I WANT.* The truck zoomed past the line of cars on its oversized tires, crushed three of the orange cones, and nearly hit a Prius as it cut into the line.

Apparently not all clowns wear makeup.

CHAPTER 2
Desert Accent

"...the creepy clown epidemic could prove to be a bit of a boon for the internet porn business, with "clown porn" searches skyrocketing in recent weeks, according to a new study from Pornhub. [...] clown-related porn searches on the popular porn site have surged by a whopping 213% since mid-September, and there have been at least 100,000 clown porn searches in the last 30 days alone."

-Tony Merevick, "Clown porn searches have skyrocketed thanks to the creepy clown epidemic," *Thrill List*, published October 14, 2016

I stopped at a truck stop diner for some lunch a few miles past Adelanto. The place had a vaguely Western theme, with whimsical wood signs on the bathroom doors that said BEST SEAT IN THE HOUSE! A rack by the cash register contained the sort of corny humor books that you find at these roadside stops. Titles like *If Life Were Fair, Horses Would Ride Half the Time* and *How to Make People Think You're Normal* offered to distract readers from the monotony of the desert road.

I sat at the counter beneath a series of television sets, all tuned to FOX News. The Muzak played a nonstop loop of country music.

"Get you a cup of coffee, darlin'?" a waitress asked in the typical "desert accent."

It's a strange phenomenon. Once you get deep enough into the desert, this faux Southern accent creeps into people's speech. You're nowhere near Mobile or Memphis, hundreds of miles from the closest Cracker Barrel or Waffle House, yet people suddenly start talking Southern.

"Coffee sounds great," I replied. "No sugar. And I'll take a chicken Caesar salad, please."

"Mmm hmm." She glanced suspiciously over her glasses before writing down my order. A quick look at the other patrons showed me that I was the only one ordering a salad. Every other plate was covered in pools of brown gravy. This was the land of starches and cream sauces, where vegetables were mere decorations.

As I sipped my coffee, a text message from a friend came in. *Hey, David, did you know there are "chat rooms" for these creepy clowns? They're all on the Deep Web, on illegal servers. They share tips on how to scare their victims. It's like a "clown cabal" or something.*

I shuddered. Whoever these clowns were, the fact that they held their meetings in the dark underbelly of the internet—sharing virtual real estate with drug traffickers and child pornographers—made them even more disturbing.

While I had my phone out, I did a little online research on my destination. I learned that a graphic novelist had lived in the Clown Motel for an entire month. Chris Sebela held a Kickstarter campaign, raised $10,000, and moved in to write a comic about the place.

His social media posts from the month he stayed there describe a mounting sense of apprehension. What most frightened him was not the ghosts or the clown decorations, but the living people he encountered: meth addicts; biker gangs; clown troupes; drunken cowboys. His cryptic diary entry for day 18 reads simply, *I am sleeping under clown sex.*

Then there was the creepy correspondence he received in the mail while there. Because he had announced online that he would be living in the Clown Motel, people started to send him anonymous packages: clown dolls and masks, ominous postcards.

One reader sent him a book about serial killer John Wayne Gacy, with the handwritten message: *SWEET DREAMS.*

Another eccentric fan sent him an old, yellowed envelope containing a crudely-drawn map to "buried treasure" in the desert, complete with coordinates. Sebela looked, in horror, at the return address—it was his own house.

He followed the map into the desert, posting on Twitter every step of the way. Once his phone started to die, though, he headed back. Social media had acted like a "lifeline," linking him to the outside world; without that connection, he felt adrift, lost, and terrified.

I glanced around at the other patrons of the diner. Were they the sort of "country people" Sebela encountered? Most of them were either truckers passing through town, or locals whom the waitresses called "sugar" and "honey" and asked about their families. Their skin was somehow pasty and sunburned at the same time, with red blotches that suggest poor circulation. The diner may have been just two hours from L.A., but it was also somehow halfway to Nashville.

I should have counted my blessings. This would be the closest thing to civilization that I would see for the rest of the day.

CHAPTER 3
"Free Coffee"

At the edge of dark, dark woods in South Carolina, children have been telling adults that a group of clowns have been trying to lure them into the cluster of trees. They say the clowns live deep in the woods, near a house by a pond.
   - *"Creepy clown sightings in South Carolina Cause a Frenzy,"* New York Times, August 31, 2016

The road pushed further into the desert, through a steep mountain pass and into a broad, flat expanse of sand punctuated by tumbleweeds and scrub brush. The occasional signs of humanity by the roadside were not comforting: a single drawer, surrounded by scattered papers and pens; the gutted shell of a car; a pile of used diapers. A child's car seat lay in the dust, tossed out the window by someone who decided they didn't need it anymore. Either because their child had a sudden growth spurt, or because the child... I shuddered to think of the explanation.

As soon as my phone showed a couple bars of reception, I called my brother. Not only would a phone conversation help pass the time, it would make the isolation feel less absolute.

After chatting with him through a long stretch of nothingness, a building suddenly appeared on the horizon. "Hey," I said, "I think I'm coming up on a town at last. I'm gonna get out and stretch my legs. There's a sign that says, *free coffee up ahead.*"

"That's a real good way to get yourself killed, brother," he replied, "stopping for that free coffee. I'll tell you what that is: that's a cannibal who preys on the weary traveler."

"No," I laughed, "I'm pretty sure it's fine."

Then my phone cut off.

A minute later, a small, faded sign announced: *NOW ENTERING RED MOUNTAIN.*

For the first couple blocks, it looked like nobody had lived in the town in years. Every storefront on Main Street had been abandoned long ago. Weeds nearly swallowed a boarded up building with chipped white paint, with an old yellow sign that read *SILVER DOLLAR SALOON*. The name "Atlantic Richfield" on the auto mechanic shop had faded to a quasi-German word: "*Allantichliebfield.*" Judging by the glass missing from its windows, the shop closed long before hybrid cars appeared on the market—probably even before power steering.

A dozen other buildings had lost any trace of the businesses that once occupied them. On either side of the street, a handful of trailers lay scattered about the desert in no particular order. My brother's comment had been a joke, of course. Still, if ever there was a town where you might expect to see a man lying in the street—and another man crouched over him eating his face off—this was it.

I finally found a long, wood-paneled building with a GENERAL STORE sign hanging over its covered porch. *This must be where the free coffee is. Looks like it's the only place in town that's open.*

I pulled into the gravel driveway and shut off my engine. Someone at the back of the house poked their head out, took a brief look at my car, and darted back inside.

A van parked inside the metal gate was covered in a collage of interesting bumper stickers. These included the callous *WORK HARDER, 15 MILLION PEOPLE ON WELFARE DEPEND ON YOU,* the popular claim to be *Not Of This World,* the spectacularly absurd *JESUS LOVES YOU; ALLAH WANTS YOU DEAD,* and the accidentally honest **ANTI-SOCIAL***ISM,* with *anti-social* highlighted in bright red.

I walked up onto the wood porch and checked the first door. A large *NO TRESPASSING* sign hung above the rusty knob. It was locked. The second door was the same. I didn't see an "open" sign anywhere on the building.

When I came to the third door, a young girl's face was pressed against the window, staring out at me. She turned and ran away when I approached. I knocked.

A woman appeared wearing a calico "pioneer" dress with a frilly white collar and wrists. She could have been one of Warren Jeffs' "sister wives," recently escaped from the Fundamentalist Mormon colony.

"Come on in," the woman said as she slowly opened the door. Her eyes remained fixed on the floor.

"Oh, uh, is this...is the free coffee..."

"Yes," she whispered, and walked away.

As my eyes adjusted to the dim light inside, I made out a series of shelves piled heavy with tools, books, and hundreds of unidentifiable knickknacks. The front shelves looked like they contained gold prospecting equipment: pans, picks, shovels, and even sluice boxes.

"Oh, hey bro," said a raspy voice behind me. "Welcome to our shop. Today's our grand opening."

I turned and saw a thin, white man dressed like he had just come from the Saint Patrick's Day parade. His button-up shirt, a brilliant shade of green, hung loose and billowy on his wiry frame. I guessed that it might be the only dress shirt he owned. Several discolored tattoos adorned his darkly tanned neck. His hair was slicked back—not in a "Gordon Gecko," 1980s stockbroker look, though. More like someone who had done some hard time.

"Thank you," I said. "I was just wondering about the free coffee..."

"Oh yeah, sure, we got it, bro." He spoke with a jumpy, nervous cadence. "But, you know, I'm sorry about that, bro, 'cause it's not hot no more, bro. But you know what I can do, bro, if it's okay, I can nuke it... Is that cool?"

He retreated to the back room. The little girl I had seen at the window now stood leaning against the frame of the kitchen doorway.

"What's your name?" I asked. She stared in silence, then disappeared again.

I walked into the second room of the shop, where a life-sized cardboard cutout of Roger Moore's James Bond greeted me. The glass case contained high-end hidden cameras, radio signal scramblers, switchblades, brass knuckles, and safes disguised to look like old tin cans of food. I expected to find a box somewhere with the label, "Paranoid Survivalist Starter Pack." Here was everything you needed to make it through the apocalypse.

I returned to the front room and looked at the bookshelves. Most of the books were about religious fundamentalism and gold mining. I wanted to peruse some of them, but a section of chain link fence lay across the shelves.

"Sorry about that," the shopkeeper said as he handed me a Styrofoam cup of coffee. "Keeps the tweakers out. I don't want some clown coming in and stealing my books, you know?"

"I can see how that would be a problem."

"There's some real nuts out there."

I told him it was about time for me to get back on the road.

"Oh, sure, no problem, bro. Thanks for stopping by." I had my hand on the doorknob, ready to leave, when he called out to me again. "Oh, one more thing..."

The man fished around for something in the pocket of his baggy slacks. *If my life were a horror movie,* I thought, *this would be the part where it looks like he's going to let me get away. I'm almost out the door, and then he whacks me over the head. Or the drugs in my coffee kick in, and I pass out. Come to think of it, that coffee did taste a little funny...*

Finally, the shopkeeper found what he was looking for: a handful of religious comic books.

"I just wanted to share these with you, bro. They changed my life. Got me back on the straight and narrow."

There were four booklets. They described the Satanic origins of Islam, homosexuality, evolution, and the Catholic Church.

"Be careful out there," he said as I got into my car.

"Thanks. I will."

I didn't finish the coffee.

CHAPTER 4
The Gods of Fear

"[T]he clown's art is now rather terrifying and full of anxiety and apprehension, their suicidal feats, their monstrous gesticulations and frenzied mimicry reminding one of the courtyard of a lunatic asylum."
-Edmond de Goncourt, French literary critic, 1876

The road out of Red Mountain cut straight into the flat, desolate expanse to the north. By 6:00 p.m., the sun painted the desert in stark chiaroscuro, black shadows contrasting with brilliant white sand. A series of rising, rolling hills in the distance reminded me of a blanket haphazardly tossed over a mess. Enormous rock formations rose abruptly from the ground, like some careless giant had left his toys lying around.

The contours of the landscape became jagged, enigmatic and menacing. A murder of crows hovered above a road sign at a fork in the road. For reasons unknown, somebody had knocked half of the sign off with a blunt object.

An antisocial act like vandalizing a road sign is easy out here in the desert, I thought. *No witnesses. In the city, on the other hand, you need a mask.*

Could this be the appeal behind the "creepy clown" phenomenon? Did hiding behind a clown outfit and makeup give certain people *carte blanche* to set their antisocial instincts loose? It certainly did for John Wayne Gacy. He relished in his clown persona "Pogo," painting self portraits of Pogo even while in prison. Before his arrest, the serial killer told police officers, "You know, clowns can get away with murder."

The highway climbed a mountain range, then descended into the industrial hell of Searles Valley. From high up, I could see the perfectly flat canvas of the desert floor stretched out, dusted with some fine, white substance. Vast expanses of pipes sectioned the flatlands off into quadrants, creating a harsh, unnatural symmetry. As I entered the valley, the towers of an industrial plant loomed above the skyline, belching thick clouds of smoke into the air. What did the factory make? Chalk? Salt? White face powder for clowns? Whatever the product, it didn't seem to have delivered on any promises of "job creation."

Searles Valley felt even more destitute than Red Mountain. A gutted "E Z Serve" service station marked the entrance to town, surrounded by the empty skeletons of houses. The general store didn't look like it had opened in years. A lone, skinny teenager rode his bike across the sand as the sun dipped behind the tall mountains to the west, casting the whole town in an oppressive shadow.

At the far end of town, the high school gymnasium had been painted with the mascot, "The Tornados." The name was fitting. Searles Valley felt like a place that had been leveled by a tornado, never to recover.

* * * *

As I drove across the rusty railroad tracks that marked the limits of Searles Valley, the sunlight was fading fast. The road turned sharply downhill. The darker it got, the more I became aware of my own mounting anxiety.

Of course, I was still excited to experience the strange Clown Motel firsthand. The mystery of the place fascinated me. As I drove deeper into the desert, however, an opposing instinct grew within me—the urge to run in the opposite direction. An inner voice told me it wasn't too late to turn the car around and drive all the way back home.

Many cultures have legends about a creature or spirit that can only be defeated by overcoming one's own fear. When I lived with the Tzotzil Mayans of southern Mexico, they told me of a fearsome specter, *Me Ixpakinté,* who haunts the woods at night. If you encounter her, you must face her with absolute courage. *Me Ixpakinté* feeds on human fear, and can suck your soul dry.

Similar traditions exist all over the world. The Huichol natives of northern Mexico say that, when embarking on the sacred journey to consume peyote in the desert, you can show no hesitation. If you confront the Dark Unknown with fear in your heart, you might go mad. The Tibetan Book of the Dead tells of a fierce wind that pulls at one's soul at the moment of death. "Do not be afraid of it!" the holy book warns. "A frightening thick darkness draws you irresistibly. You are terrified by harsh cries, such as 'Strike!' 'Kill!' Do not be afraid of them!"

Maybe these are all different names for the same enemy—fear itself. Fear cannot be escaped; it needs to be confronted.

Of course, this was not the first time I would visit a haunted place to write about it. And yet, I had the growing sense that this time, I might be in over my head.

I thought back to that day at Disneyland when I was five, surrounded by the mocking, painted smiles. I recalled the gruesome face that popped up from behind the tombstone. That was all just an amusement park, of course. Whatever awaited me at the Clown Motel, on the other hand—well, that was real life. And I was going to face it on my own.

In addition to the childhood fears that crept into my mind—the clowns, the dark, the unknown—a much more practical concern loomed: I would be hours from the nearest city. I might not have any cell phone reception. For all I knew, there might not be any police in Tonopah. And I would be staying at a Clown Motel at the height of *actual clown sightings.*

Whoever these "creepy clowns" are, a clown-themed motel might draw them in. Hell, it would be like a Mecca for them.

These were the thoughts running through my mind as the last rays of sunlight vanished, when a sign announced: *NOW ENTERING DEATH VALLEY.*

CHAPTER 5
Death Valley

"The legend says that every spirit must pass through there on the way to perfection. There, you will meet your own shadow self... But, it is said, if you confront the Black Lodge with imperfect courage, it will utterly annihilate your soul."
 -Deputy Hawk, *Twin Peaks*

Plunged into the pure blackness of a moonless, starless night, I realized how weak my headlights really were. They only managed to illuminate a few yards of road ahead. A fierce wind blew across the desert, howling through the open spaces and nudging my car enough to keep me on edge. It also dragged the dust across the road in thin, undulating snakes. The twisting, shifting lines of sand swelled, rippled and curved, disorienting me and making my head ache.

The dizzying effect of these dust storms was increased by the fact that the road contained no reflectors or signs of any kind. No markers to indicate the edge of the highway. No guard rails. I hadn't seen a streetlight since I left Adelanto hours ago. Just me and the morphing, ever-changing surface of the highway, surrounded by absolute darkness. This was the sort of experience that was created especially for those of us who have never tried psychedelic drugs.

After an hour driving across the flat expanse of Death Valley, the one-lane highway climbed the steep mountains to the east. If the previous hour had been disorienting, the second leg of the journey was pure terror. The road curved and snaked around cliffs, ledges, hills, and steep, jagged drops. With no warning, a hairpin turn appeared suddenly, making me slam on the breaks and squint into the darkness beyond it. Every couple miles, the harrowing scene repeated itself. I slowed to 40 MPH, then 30, then 15.

My mind was pushed into a heightened state of alertness where I could see no further than the two seconds immediately ahead of me, always trying to keep from plummeting off a cliff and into the darkness, where every demon from my childhood nightmares lay waiting.

I began to pray.

I promised God that I would devote the rest of my life to goodwill and charity, if He would just get me out of there in one piece. I thought about all the people I loved and longed to see again. The memory of their faces and voices slowly slipped away from me.

I started to feel like my entire life before that moment had been a cruel illusion. I had always been in that black valley, since before the dawn of time, and I would stay there for all eternity. It was like an evil version of the present-minded consciousness that Zen Buddhists talk about. I began to give up hope. I was in Sheol, the eternal shadowland of the dead.

Just when I was ready to park my car in the desert and cry myself to sleep, I saw lights ahead. Streetlights! Humans; a real human settlement!

The town of Beatty welcomed me with all the opulent luxuries of modern life: gas stations, houses, a hotel, a public library, a restaurant. If I had seen it immediately after leaving San Diego, I would have probably called it a dismal, Podunk town. After surviving Death Valley, however, I was ready to kneel down and kissed the oily asphalt of its streets.

* * * *

I ate dinner at Beatty's only restaurant. A sunburned man in his 60s sat with his wife sat a couple seats down the counter.

"I see you're writing." The man nodded toward my notebook. He had a drooping, gray moustache and a cowboy slouch.

"Just taking a few notes. On my way to Tonopah."

"Yep, I know the place." He spoke with the same "desert accent" I'd noticed earlier that day, at the diner in Adelanto. "Tonopah. That's about two more hours up the road."

I told him and his wife about the Clown Motel, its reputation for being haunted, and my plan to spend three nights there.

"There's certainly something about a lot of these old mining towns," the woman said with gravity. "Strange things have been known to happen here."

"I think it's the history of the place." The man's Sam Elliott moustache puffed in and out as he spoke, his matching eyebrows furrowing low over his eyes. "The Old West. They found gold or silver on a little patch of desert, and suddenly five or ten thousand people all pack into that tiny little space. Folks would fight for land, claims, money, women. They got stabbed or shot, or suffocated in the mines. All that murder and death has a way of . . . sticking to a place."

I paid my bill, said goodbye to the couple, and got back on the road. A faint drizzle fell as I left Beatty. A green sign announced the next towns down the road:

TONOPAH: 95 MILES

RENO: 330 MILES

The signs hadn't made any omissions. During the entire two hours of cold desert highway, I saw nothing but the rain and the black night. At least the road was flat.

Around midnight, when my eyelids were growing heavy from the journey, I reached Tonopah. The silent, boarded up buildings of downtown were entirely dark. Finally, a faint light glimmered at the distant the edge of town. Two white halogen lights shone on a mostly empty parking lot with an unlit sign towering over it. Even in the dark, I could make out the shape of a painted face, blood red lips, gloved hands, and three juggled balls hovering in the air. The sign announced to the dark, silent desert:

CLOWN MOTEL.

CHAPTER 6
The Motel

"Can't sleep... Clown'll eat me... Can't sleep... Clown'll eat me..."
-Bart Simpson

The clock on my car's dashboard read 12:27 a.m. I parked and stepped out into the freezing desert night. A harsh wind bit at my skin and dragged tears from my eyes. I pulled a heavy jacket from my trunk and took a look at my surroundings.

The motel consisted of two long, two-story buildings in an L-shape, all the doors opening onto the central parking lot. An outdoor walkway connected the rooms, bordered by a weather-worn wood railing. On the ground floor of one building, a hand-painted Lobby sign with two clowns welcomed me.

"Well, this is it," I said to the cold night sky. "Time to check in. I'm at the mercy of the clowns, now."

I crunched across the gravel parking lot, walking slowly, like the main character in a prison movie when he first enters The Yard. The lobby window was entirely dark. I knocked a couple times on the Plexiglas door.

"Hello? Anybody in there?"

I cupped my hands against the cold window and peered inside. A life-sized clown statue stared back at me from the shadows. A sign taped to the glass announced:

LOBBY CLOSES AT 11 P.M. CALL THIS NUMBER FOR EMERGENCIES.

I dialed it. After six rings, an exhausted woman's voice answered.

"Hello?"

"Um...yes, I had a reservation for tonight."

"We close at...okay, just wait a second," she croaked.

She came down the nearby staircase five minutes later in a faded bathrobe—bleary-eyed, with long, graying blonde hair.

"Reception closes at eleven." She said it matter-of-factly, as if anyone would be insane to expect a motel to be open at nighttime.

"Sorry, I didn't know," I said. "Could I bother you for the key, though?"

The woman thought for a second, then grunted assent. She fished in her pocket, handed me a bronze key, and pointed out my room on the second floor.

"You can come into the lobby and pay us tomorrow."

"Thank you so much. I'm sorry to have woken you up."

The staircase was covered with dirty, weather-worn Astroturf, like an abandoned miniature golf course. I glanced down the walkway at the other rooms. Every door contained a painted plywood cutout of a different clown. Some laughed, some cried. Some simply bared their teeth in a primal, animal gesture of aggression.

I turned the key in the stiff lock and pushed the door open with my shoulder.

The smell of stale cigarettes hung in the dark room. This was the kind of motel where the idea of a "non-smoking room" is pointless. The floor issued exaggerated creaks with every step I took, like the over-the-top effects from an old horror movie. I turned on the light on the nightstand.

"Holy shit!"

I shouted. I jumped back. A three-foot-tall clown painting stared down at me from the wall opposite the bed.

The orange-haired figure wore an old-fashioned European clown outfit, like Pagliacci from the eponymous opera. His features had been painted with rough, irregular lines. While his mouth smiled with smug cockiness, his eyes said, "I'll kick your ass if you laugh at me."

This was the face I would wake up to for the next three days.

I took a walk around the room. The uneven, mauve carpet bubbled up at the edges of the floor. Corners of the ceiling had swollen with water damage. All the furniture seemed to have been made from the same leftover plywood scraps. The shower contained a lower ledge to sit on, its surface worn gray over the years by a thousand bare asses.

The remote control on the dresser didn't work. I manually turned on the TV's stiff metal switch, and discovered that it got a total of zero stations. It was the sort of model that we had when I was a kid in the 1980s, a bulky cube as deep as it was wide. When I shut it off after a minute of white fuzz, a faint, colored blob appeared on the dark screen. My brother and I used to call this TV residue "the ghost."

I headed down the creaky outdoor stairs to collect my belongings from my car: one backpack, one laptop, a copy of Stephen King's *IT*—and my baseball bat.

* * * *

Driving through the black night of Death Valley had left me thoroughly exhausted. When I disrobed and laid down on the bed, I expected to fall into a deep sleep. I was not so lucky.

The thin curtains did little to block out the light from the halogen bulb on the porch. It cast a soft glow over the clown painting at the foot of my bed. The cold desert wind made the old building creak and groan. I found it difficult to sleep for more than two or three minutes at a time.

I have often heard of people suffering from "sleep paralysis." According to psychologists, this occurs when a person's body falls asleep from exhaustion, but their mind becomes stuck in an in-between state. That first night in the clown motel, I think I experienced it for the first time.

It felt like I was in a limbo of consciousness, half asleep and half awake. Sounds and images floated up from my unconscious mind and bled into reality. Just when I barely managed to fall asleep, a loud sound from a dream jarred me awake, and I would look around the room in panic.

At one point, I heard a voice calling my name, right next to my pillow. *"David, David... DAVID."* When it shouted in my ear, I sat bolt upright—it had been my own voice.

Then there were the real noises. The symphony of macabre, eerie sounds echoing throughout the motel kept me in a constant state of agitation. The 95 highway was close enough for me to hear every 18-wheeler that whooshed past. Fierce gusts of wind howled through the Tonopah Valley. Any time another guest walked to the bathroom, the whole building creaked loudly. At 2:27 a.m., a new sound woke me up—an otherworldly moaning.

It was rhythmic and regular, punctuated by periods of silence. *"Uuuuhnnn."* Break. *"Uuuuhnnn."* Break. *"Uuuuhnnn."* Break.

My half-dreaming mind twisted and distorted the voice, giving it an inhuman air. Once I got up to go to the bathroom, I finally recognized it as the sound a man snoring. The guest in the room next to mine had a bizarre way of vocalizing the out-breath when he snored, which created the strange moaning:

(Inhale) *"Trrrr..."* (Exhale) *"Uuuuhnnn."* (Inhale) *"Trrrr..."* (Exhale) *"Uuuuhnnn."*

I willed myself unconscious again. Over the next hour, I had some of the most horrifying dreams of my life.

These were the recurrent nightmares that haunted my childhood, the sort of personalized fears that everyone has lodged deep in their skull. They all resurfaced that night. Monsters from the briny deeps of the ocean. Invisible demons hiding in the shadows. Helplessness in the face of danger. Murder, gore, assault.

I thought of the scene in Stephen King's *IT* where the "Losers' Club" meets up as adults, and the monster terrorizes them at the restaurant. Each person sees the thing they are most afraid of on their plate—a giant insect, an eyeball, a spray of blood—a tailor-made horror just for them.

Most of my dreams from that night were so intimate, so personal, that I would never write them down in a book intended for the general public. Suffice it to say that my dreams were as terrifying for me as the reader's darkest nightmares are for him or her. I wondered if the Clown Motel was the kind of special place that that conjures up a unique, personalized Hell for every individual.

Around three o'clock in the morning, another ambient noise woke me up. Someone was walking back and forth in the room above me.

Go back to sleep, I told myself. *It's just some insomniac walking around his room.*

I clearly heard each one of the neighbor's steps creaking across the ceiling above me, left to right to left to right.

Who knows why he's awake at three in the morning? Not my problem.

Creak, creak, creak. Back and forth, slow and rhythmic.

The floors in this place make a lot of noise. There's nothing I can do about it. Just go back to sleep.

Then the realization hit me:

My room is on the top floor. There aren't *any other rooms above me.*

I sat up, eyes wide open, mind fully awake. I could still hear the creaking footsteps.

After they subsided, it took an hour for me to get back to sleep. I normally sleep on my side with my arms and legs sprawled out. When I awoke the following morning, however, I found myself curled in the fetal position.

THREE NIGHTS IN THE CLOWN MOTEL

CHAPTER 7

An Infestation of Clowns

Never shall I forget the repulsive sight that met my eye when I turned round. He was dressed for the pantomimes in all the absurdity of a clown's costume. The spectral figures in the Dance of Death, the most frightful shapes that the ablest painter ever portrayed on canvas, never presented an appearance half so ghastly. His bloated body and shrunken legs—their deformity enhanced a hundredfold by the fantastic dress—the glassy eyes, contrasting fearfully with the thick white paint with which the face was besmeared; the grotesquely-ornamented head, trembling with paralysis, and the long skinny hands, rubbed with white chalk—all gave him a hideous and unnatural appearance, of which no description could convey an adequate idea, and which, to this day, I shudder to think of.
    -Charles Dickens, *The Pickwick Papers*

I awoke feeling groggy and disoriented, like all the worst parts of a hangover without any of the fun. I pulled on my sport pants and sweatshirt and headed outdoors. Maybe a morning jog would clear my head.

A cold, uninviting wind froze my face as I stepped out onto the Astroturf of the motel's porch. It was much colder than I had expected. I knew Tonopah was in the desert, but I hadn't checked its altitude. This was the high desert country where it snowed in the winter, where corpses buried in December didn't finish decomposing until June.

I squinted into the harsh morning sunlight and took a look at my surroundings. The sky was a uniform, flat gray, the color of gunmetal. To the north, the highway stretched off into the flat desert. This truly was the edge of town. *I don't know if I want to go running around the wilderness. Coyotes, scorpions, rattlesnakes... I'll take my chances with that trailer park to the south.*

I started jogging down the cracked asphalt of the highway and up the first side street. The road quickly turned into a dirt path that twisted and curved uphill into a residential area. A motley scattering of old trailers covered the dusty foothills, all faded paint and rusty edges, every door and window shut. Not a soul walking around outside. It was hard to tell how many of these trailers were even inhabited—many of the windows had been boarded up and the yards left to decay. Fifteen minutes into my jog, I saw the first and only car crawling down the narrow dirt road. The tinted windows hid its passengers from sight.

A cross street with the menacing name of "Cutting Road" led me to the outskirts of the small neighborhood. The only permanent wood houses appeared to have been abandoned long ago. Three mangy dogs barked at me from behind a rusty chain link fence. I guessed they had never seen a person running for any legitimate reason before.

Despite the cold wind stinging my face, I was working up a sweat. I followed the dirt road up into the barren hills west of town. I slowed to a walk when I noticed something glittering in the dirt. The sand sparkled for miles around, glistening in the early morning light. Hundreds of glass bottles and rusty metal scraps lay all around. Old springs, pots, twisted and jagged shards.

I bent to pick up a dark green bottle. The cut was rougher and the glass much thicker than a modern bottle. These hills must have been a junkyard back when this was a booming mining town, when humans rushed here by the thousands to seek their fortune. Now this was all that remained—miles of trash, the rusty fragments of a society long gone, all their owners dead and beneath the ground.

It was like visiting the end of the world.

* * * *

Back at the motel, I showered and went down to the lobby to pay for my first night. A half dozen cars were parked in the lot, which was six more than I would have expected to see at a Clown Motel in the desert.

The bells hanging from the lobby door jingled when I pushed it open. I blinked in the dim light.

I was surrounded by them. The clowns.

To say that there were "a lot" of them doesn't quite capture it. While it would be numerically accurate to say the lobby contained over 600 clown dolls, this would also fail to properly capture the horror of the place. *Infestation* would be a good word. The lobby was *infested* with clowns.

The first one to greet me was an enormous, shiny Ronald McDonald statue just inside the door. His faded, glazed eyes stared at me inscrutably, his red mouth curled into a smile. He held up a white gloved hand.

I walked past Ronald and saw hundreds of his clown brothers staring down at me from all sides. Stacked on the shelves, dangling from the ceiling, arranged on the floor. *Our name is Legion, for we are many,* they seemed to say.

Porcelain figurines with delicate features. Plush dolls with rainbow hair. A sad "hobo clown" with a five o'clock shadow. A horned clown face with a handkerchief body, dangling from a nail on the shelf. Grotesque features, deformed hands and feet, mocking grins.

The receptionist from the previous night stood behind the desk, chatting on the phone. *How can she remain so calm,* I thought, *when surrounded by these creatures?*

A plastic cage on the desk contained a quintessential "evil clown" doll—red eyes, fangs, claws. This one didn't even bother me. I was much more disturbed by the clowns with sly, cocky grins on their faces. An evil-looking clown just makes me think of cheap, B-horror films. The quiet, smug grin, however, can only mean one thing: *This clown is real, and he dreams about murder all day long.*

The receptionist acknowledged my presence with a nod and continued her phone conversation. I stared up at the signed clown photographs behind the desk. One black-and-white clown grinned psychotically, hair disheveled, eyes promising violence and chaos. I took a few steps backwards and bumped into something. It creaked. I turned.

A high, girlish shriek escaped my throat.

I had bumped into a rocking chair containing the ugliest mannequin I had ever seen. He wore a sheen fabric costume of rainbow stripes, with a matching conical hat. Aside from the red pompom, it could have been a Klansman's hood. His wooden hands had been painted with eerie realism—detailed knuckles and veins and bones. I squinted, fancying the possibility that they were real, dehydrated human hands.

And the face. Oh God, the face. It was a smooth, waxen figure of indeterminate age. The corners of its crimson mouth turned gently upward, its eyes half-shut in opioid glee. It was the smug smile of Zen-peace-meets-psychopathy.

"Can I help you?" The receptionist held one hand over the receiver.

"I just need to pay for last night. I'm in room twelve."

She slid the credit card machine across the counter and went back to the phone. I decided I'd ask about the rocking chair clown later on—this was all too much to handle on an empty stomach. I signed the receipt and headed out into the cold morning air, giving one last look over my shoulder.

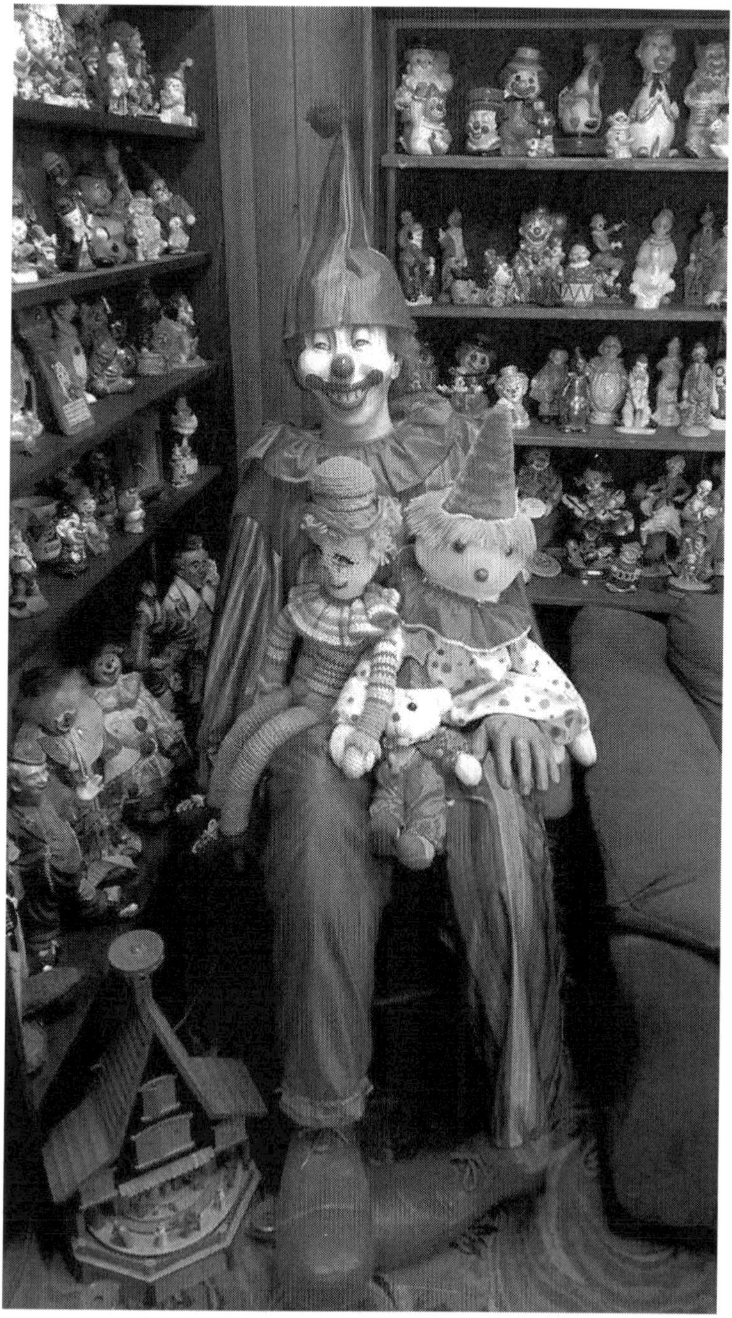

CHAPTER 8
Voices in the Graveyard

"Marlene Warren was at her home on May 26, 1990, when she answered her front door and was met by a clown carrying a flower arrangement and two balloons, who offered the items to her. Witnesses said they heard a gunshot and Marlene Warren fell to the ground. The clown then walked back to a vehicle in the driveway. Marlene Warren was hospitalized and died two days later."

-David Caplan, "Police Arrest Woman in 'Killer Clown' Cold Case," *Good Morning America*, published September 27, 2017

A defeated mood hung over the Main Street of Tonopah. Heavy gray clouds lay low, unmoved by the freezing wind that howled past.

I drove slowly, looking for a place to eat. Most of the windows were boarded up. The only building that looked open was a red brick structure with the cryptic word *MIZPAH* on the front. It sounded like the sort of place you would rent out for your son's Bar Mitzvah. The occasional parked car was the only real sign of life. I began to feel like my search for breakfast would turn up hopeless

Finally, a sign on the horizon announced, in sparkling lights: *CASINO, RESTAURANT, HOTEL*. I predicted that this would be my main source of food over the next couple days. The large dark wood building sat in an expansive strip mall of mostly empty storefronts.

After the sparseness of Main Street—not to mention the place where I was lodged—this hotel felt incredibly luxurious. Dark-stained wood paneling covered every surface, with the fancy maroon carpet of some bygone era. Taxidermied bears and wolves lined the hallway, which divided the lobby and gift shop on the left from the casino on the right. It felt like something you would find in an historic mining town that got a lot of tourism, like Virginia City, with Old West re-enactors and buggy rides and sarsaparilla. This hotel must have been built in anticipation of a golden age of tourism that never came to Tonopah.

I walked into the casino area, with the familiar smell of smoke and electronic *ching ching ching chings*, and sat down to play a little video poker before breakfast. Other than a thin, clean-shaven white man in his thirties at the other end of the communal table, the place was empty.

"You on your way to Reno or Vegas?" he asked me.

"Neither. I came here on purpose."

He laughed. "What'd you do that for?"

When I told him I came to experience the Clown Motel, he shook his head and glanced downward. "No way, man. Not in a million years. Not for a million bucks could you get me to stay there. Creepy as hell."

I asked if he had been born in Tonopah. He explained that he moved out from California several years ago, to get off drugs and seek a fresh start. He had found a job working in one of the few mines still open in the region.

"So what's it like living here?" I asked.

"This town is...different." He cashed out and left.

I withdrew my $5 winnings and walked through the casino to the diner. Old West wood paneling and vintage wallpaper covered the walls, between windows of stained glass. Antique Coca-Cola and cigarette ads hung everywhere. One poster stuck out to me—advertising "Punch soda," it depicted a vintage joker clown holding a bottle. I remembered where I would be sleeping that night.

Two waitresses worked the place: one heavy-set brunette with a French braid, and a woman in her sixties with a ponytail of long, sandy blonde hair.

"Did you hear about this robbery in Vegas?" The older waitress spoke with the "desert accent" I had come to expect.

"Which one?" her coworker with the French braid asked.

"The guys wearing the animal masks! It's been on the news all morning." The older woman's jaw thrust forward she spoke. "A bunch of them stormed into one of those high-end jewelry stores with their masks on, all of 'em carrying sledgehammers. They smashed the jewelry cases and took off with whatever they could get their hands on. The woman behind the desk just screamed the whole time, staring at the animal masks and the hammers."

"Boy, I'm glad that's six hours away," the younger girl said as she filled the coffee machine with fresh grounds. "I thought you meant the *other* story about an attack in Vegas. The guy who held up that double-decker bus on the Strip. He fired some shots and held the passengers hostage. I guess the cops are still in a standoff with him. They've got the whole Strip shut down; they're not letting any traffic in or out."

"You know," said the older waitress shaking her head, "sometimes I feel like the whole world's gone crazy."

I took my seat at the worn oak counter beneath an enormous, antique copper pot hanging from the ceiling. The radio played an old 1940s country song by Bob Wills, *The Devil Ain't Lazy*.

"What can I get you, honey?" asked the older waitress. She had the easy-going, friendly demeanor of a bartender. I ordered the ham steak and eggs, with extra hash browns. She poured me a cup of coffee without even asking, likely noticing the heavy circles under my eyes.

"So I guess this is pretty much the only restaurant in town?" I asked when she came back from the kitchen.

"Oh no, it's far from the only one."

"What other restaurants are there?"

"Well, I mean, there's... Well, there's a Burger King by the gas station. That's over on the other end of town."

"By the Clown Motel?"

She chuckled. "Heck of a place, huh? Have you seen it?"

"I'm staying there."

The country singer on the radio crooned about the Devil eliciting moans and groans with his pitchfork.

"Wow!" The waitress said. "So... How is the Clown Motel? I mean, we've had a few folks come get a room over here after spending a night here. They say it's... Well, they say this place is a little nicer."

"It's not without its charm." I forced a smile. "So what do you think... Is it true what they say? Do you think it's haunted?"

"Let me tell you, darlin', in a town like this, nearly *every* place is haunted."

She left to check on her other tables. I started sorting through my photos of the clown dolls in the lobby.

"You know," the waitress said when she returned with my food, "I used to work as a bartender at the Mizpah hotel downtown."

"Is that the big, red brick building on Main Street?" I asked.

"Yeah, that's it. It's been here since the old mining days, and the strangest things would happen in there. For instance, there was this one guest who was having a drink in the bar. He said goodnight and headed up to his room. A minute later, he came back down—he couldn't get into his room."

"Maybe his key got demagnetized?" I suggested.

"Thing is, they don't have any of those new-fangled electronic key cards at the Mizpah. It's all metal keys. He came back down to the bar and said, 'Somebody locked my door.' I asked if he had his room key on him, and he said, 'No, it's the deadbolt that's locked.' And those deadbolts only lock from the *inside*. Management had a heck of a time getting his door open. I guess somebody—or something—really didn't want him in that room."

"Wow. Sounds like some poltergeist activity." I told her that I had come to Tonopah looking for ghost stories. In the background, the song on the radio warned listeners not to act too strong or too brave—the Devil, after all, isn't lazy.

"Well, if you're looking for ghosts," the waitress said, "the Clown Motel is a good place to find them. I have a niece who went there one night with some of her girlfriends. They're about fifteen, and they wanted to do some 'ghost hunting.' They took a recorder with them and kept it running the whole time. Trying to see if they could catch any 'spirit voices.'"

"So did they?"

"They played the recording for me. Nobody talking or anything, but... I did hear something. About twenty minutes into the recording, when they were inside one of the hotel rooms. It sounded like something... growling."

My eyes opened wide.

"Right, that's the look I made!" she said. "The growling only lasted a few seconds when they were in the motel. But then they went down to that old graveyard, and it came back. It got so loud, you couldn't even hear the girls' voices on the recording—just that deep, deep growl."

While she tended to the other customers, I turned my phone back on to upload some photos. I had promised creepy clowns to the people of the internet, and I had to deliver. I pulled up a picture of the life-sized clown in the rocking chair—the one with the smug smile and the realistic wooden hands—and set my phone down on the counter to grab a napkin.

Before I could hit the *upload* button, the phone scrolled over to the next photo. On its own, without my touching it. The next picture came up, and the next one. The phone scrolled through my images on its own, as if someone were swiping their invisible fingers across the screen over and over again. Both my hands were a good three feet from it.

"What's the matter, sir?" The waitress stood behind me, poised to take my empty plate. "You look like somebody just walked over your grave."

"I… I think I'll take the check now."

CHAPTER 9
Paint on His Face and Spikes on His Teeth

"We found that clowns are universally disliked by children. Some found them quite frightening and unknowable."
-Dr. Penny Curtis, University of Sheffield

I headed back to the motel to take a look around the old cemetery next door. I checked my phone as I drove back down the Main Street of Tonopah. When I saw that it was working again, I gave my dad a call.

"Where are you calling from, Davey?" He asked. "You sound fuzzy."

"The middle of the Nevada desert. At a haunted Clown Motel. Don't tell Mom, though—not until I get back alive. I don't want her to worry too much."

As I described the motel over the phone, I pulled into its parking lot and got out of the car. The late afternoon light bathed the neon sign in a soft, orange glow. I walked across the lot toward the graveyard.

"Hey," my dad said, "did I ever tell you about the clown dream I had as a kid?"

I stood in front of the wrought iron gateway to the cemetery. "Remind me again."

"I was, oh, probably five or six. But I can still remember the dream perfectly. I was at the gas station near our house. I walked up to this big pickup truck parked at one of the pumps, with a tall man in coveralls standing by it. The man turned around, and his face was painted like a clown. He looked a lot like Bozo, with the white makeup and red lips, but his hair was shorter, almost bald. Had a big, striped hat on."

My dad might have been describing the life-sized clown doll in the motel lobby. I leaned against the cemetery gate and listened more closely.

"The clown smiled at me. He peeled his lips back, and he had these big metal spikes coming off his teeth. 'Look what ya made me do, kid.' His voice was like a growl. 'Ya made me spill the gaaaaaas…'"

My dad's voice cut out. The phone had lost all signal.

The sinking sun cast long, black shadows behind the tombstones. I crunched across the gravelly soil, stepping carefully around each grave. Most of them were marked with simple rock outlines and wooden headstones. A few of them described the cause of death:

STABBED

SHOT IN BACK

DIED IN MINE EXPLOSION

Natural death was a rare thing in old Tonopah.

The cold desert wind howled across the dry earth, blowing up dust devils, rustling the weeds that grew at the edge. I shivered. I hadn't brought my jacket. The shadows of four or five tombstones at the far edge of the cemetery overlapped, forming the shape of a long, distorted hand stretched towards me. I decided to leave before night fell.

I moved sluggishly up the dirty Astroturf stairs, feeling the weight of a ten-hour journey followed by a sleepless night. A nap was sounding nice—until I entered my room and saw the clown painting on the wall. Suddenly I didn't feel like sleeping anymore.

Memories of the previous night came back to me. The chilling sound of my own voice, calling out my name next to my ear. The dreams that poked their heads up from the black, loamy soil of childhood. The face behind the tombstone. The clowns.

Normally, dreams have a way of fading away as you go about your day, dissipating like so much mist. This was not the case with the nightmares brought on by the Clown Motel. They only grew more solid with time, more real.

Then there was the sound that had not come from my dreams—the inexplicable footsteps walking across the ceiling.

I sat at the table by the window and turned on my laptop. Surprised to find the motel's WiFi was actually working, I did a little more research on the recent "clown sightings."

Some of the videos were obviously staged. The college boys who uploaded one of them would have done well to take some acting classes. They filmed a clown from their car at night, then got out and attacked it. As they knocked it to the ground, they shouted such authentic teenage slang as, "Let's take a photograph of him, fellows!" I chuckled as I remembered the "Crazy Joe Davola" episode of *Seinfeld,* when a bunch of neighborhood toughs accost Joe in Central Park, melodramatically taunting, "Make us laugh, clown!"

Other videos were much more convincing.

One of the earliest clown sightings to surface online was recorded *in absentia.* The owner of a house in Jacksonville, Florida checked their security footage one day to see a menacing clown standing on their front porch. In the video, the clown stares into the security camera, head cocked to one side. His face is painted with sharp angles and a menacing smile. He picks up a Jack-o'-lantern from the porch, punches it repeatedly, bashes it in, and rips it to shreds. The clown stares into the camera for a minute and walks away. No motive or suspects were ever found.

In Texas, a home security camera captured a clown at 2:00 a.m., in full dress and makeup, armed with a butcher knife. He walks up to the front door and stares at it. He jiggles the knob. Then he turns and saunters back down the driveway. Other cameras show the clown surveying the perimeter of the property, slowly and methodically checking every gate.

Clown sightings are not limited to the United States. A Snapchat video uploaded by a girl from Canada shows a rural roadside area in British Columbia. The girl films the woods by the road, saying that somebody is standing in the darkness. As she slowly drives by, a clown darts out of the brush and rushes at her car swinging a long, blunt object.

On October 2, someone in Quebec uploaded a video of a remote, dirt road. Two young men are discussing a figure emerging from the brush: a clown in a puffy white costume. He stares at them, then wanders back into the wilderness. The men in the car remain calm. The clown suddenly comes back. He's holding a chainsaw. He fires it up and chases after them, causing the boys to drive away cursing *"Putain!"* repeatedly. If the video is a fake, it's a convincing one.

I took a break from YouTube and looked up some articles on the phenomenon. Some authors suggest that we fear clowns because we fear the human darkness that could be hiding behind the mask. When there is no human identity, there is no morality. When there is no more I, there is only "it."

I remembered reading some of Sigmund Freud's original writings in German. The terms "Id, Ego, and Superego" that we use in the English-speaking world were inserted into Freud's work by his first translators. The original German word for the Id, though—the base, animal instincts, the amoral drives, hunger, aggression, sexuality—was simply *das Es*. The It. I noted that it was also the name Stephen King gave to his killer clown.

I went back to YouTube and came across a vintage video that brought me right back to the clowns of my childhood. Someone uploaded a Disneyland commercial from 1986, advertising their circus-themed summer event. Under the appropriately creepy title, "Circus Fantasy," the announcer invites park guests to experience

"A colossal menagerie of elephants, clowns, and acrobats, in an awe-inspiring, death-defying, breathtaking, spellbinding Disney extravaganza." The commercial ends with a shot of a sneering clown painting a child's face. The clown is relishing in the chance to make a new convert, with all the zeal of a zombie or vampire biting a fresh victim.

I looked at the clown painting on the wall, staring enigmatically back at me. At that moment, I felt incredibly alone. I was a day's drive away from home. Even if I wanted to bail on this whole Clown Motel project, sundown was just a few hours away. It would be dark before I even reached Death Valley. Leaving was not an option.

In an effort to connect with to the outside world, I uploaded a video about my experience thus far. (This, and all other videos, are available in YouTube links at the end of this book.)

"I'm really not looking forward to spending another night here," I confessed. "I got a terrible night's sleep. And, of course," I pointed at the clown painting behind me, "it doesn't help that I've got this frickin' asshole staring down at me."

The effect of talking to the cold eye of my laptop's camera was the opposite of what I had hoped for. Discussing the clowns out loud, on their "home turf," made me feel apprehensive. As if they could hear me. The nightmares felt even more real.

Opting for a more personal connection with the outside world. I started writing an email to my brother:

> *This place is creepier than I had expected. I'm sorry if I ever made fun of you for being afraid of clowns.*

When I tried to hit send, the internet cut out.

DAVID J. SCHMIDT

CHAPTER 10
Twisted Faces

Crazy Joe Davola: "You ever been to the circus?"
Kramer: "Well... When I was a kid."
Crazy Joe Davola: "Did you like it?"
Kramer: "Well, you know, it was fun... I was kind of scared of the clowns."
Crazy Joe Davola: "Are you still scared of clowns?"
Kramer: "Yeah..."
  -*Seinfeld*, "The Opera"

I headed down to the lobby that evening to see if there was any coffee left in the pot. A silver-haired man in a denim jacket and jeans, a weather-worn baseball cap on his head, stood chatting with the woman behind the desk.

"This shooter has been on the news all day," the man said, looking over his shoulder at the TV behind him. The anchor discussed the man who had held up a double-decker bus in Las Vegas.

"Yeah, they just confirmed that he killed a couple people on that bus," the receptionist said. This was the first time I had seen her. She was a middle-aged woman with curly red hair and a pale complexion. Lines of concern drew across her forehead as she spoke. "He's up on the second story of the bus. The Strip's been shut down for five hours. They're shooting concussion grenades into the bus now."

"Seems this sort of thing is happening more and more these days," the man in the denim jacket said. "I don't know what's becoming of this world."

I introduced myself to the red-haired receptionist and paid for my second night. She told me her name was Maggie.

"Yep," the man continued, "seems like people just don't know how to live in society any more. Honestly, it doesn't surprise me that people elected Trump. Don't get me wrong, I'm no fan of Hillary either. But Trump... Well, it's like he's a cheerleader for the meanest, nastiest kind of people. And now," he waved at the TV, "the nuts are just coming out of the woodwork."

When Maggie left us for the laundry room, I sat on the old sofa and chatted with the man in the denim jacket, whose name was Jack. Now that the initial shock of the clowns had worn off, I took in some of the finer details of the lobby. The fake wood paneling was the kind that you might see inside a trailer where a rural Baptist church met once a week. Years of sunlight and foot traffic had faded the gaudy floral print of the carpet beyond recognition.

I asked Jack how long he had been staying in the Clown Motel.

"Just over a year."

"You're kidding me!"

"My wife and I, we've been here a year now. They give us a special discount rate, of course, as long-term guests. We're kind of in between places right now."

"What does it feel like, living in the Clown Motel full time?"

"Well, they let us redecorate the room, of course, so we've got it set up like an ordinary apartment. We've got our books and DVDs, and some of our furniture. It feels nice and homey in there now. Plus, we got rid of those god-awful clown paintings a long time ago.

"Smart move."

"My wife hates clowns, you see."

"You're kidding me!" I laughed. "And she lives at a Clown Motel??"

"Yeah, funny how things work out."

"I don't know how she does it. I can barely stand the thought of being here for another two nights."

"She really doesn't mind," he said. "But she refuses to come in here, into the lobby."

"So she prefers for you to come pay the rent?"

"She doesn't just 'prefer' it, she insists on it. She hasn't set foot in here."

A gust of wind howled outside, and the tiny motel lobby groaned in protest.

"Are you serious?" I stared, incredulous. "Not once, after more than a year?"

"Not once. That's how scared of clowns she is." He pulled out his phone and held it up. "One day, I came in here and took some pictures of a few of the dolls—the nice ones, the cute-looking ones—to show them to her. I went back to our room. 'See here, honey?' I said. 'Look at these friendly little guys. This is what you've been so scared of this whole time.'

"I handed her the phone. She made a disgusted face. 'What is this supposed to be,' she says, 'a joke? What the hell is this??' She held it up, and I couldn't believe my eyes."

A dog barked in the distance outside.

"What was in the photo?" I asked quietly.

"You couldn't make out any of the clowns' faces. In every single picture, the face was twisted, blurred, or distorted. Like someone had gone in on Photoshop and messed with the faces."

I told him about the diner earlier that day, when my phone scrolled through the pictures on its own.

"Yeah, my phone does that all the time," he said. "Ever since we came here."

"Do you think there could be something about these mountains here?" I asked. "Some kind of weird magnetism, from all the minerals in the soil here? You know, the mines and all that, the earth metals..."

"Maybe." He scratched the stubble on his chin. "I go through phones so fast. I still haven't been able to get a phone to work properly here. Lots of the other guests tell me the same thing. You know what's funny, though... I realized after awhile that my phone always starts malfunctioning when I'm *in here, in the lobby*. Like, it will work fine outside. But once I'm in here with all these clowns, it just goes nuts. It was months before I could ever get a decent photo of one of these dolls."

"Do you believe the rumors about this place?" I asked. "That it's haunted?"

"You know, brother, I've been living here a year now. And let me tell you," Jack leaned forward, "they're not just rumors."

CHAPTER 11
Mass Graves

"They had clown masks on and purge masks on," said Jeff Brown. "(They had a) knife, hockey sticks, they had clubs, they had bats." The victim said he told the women to drive away and get help. The attackers were described by the victim as teens wearing masks from the movie "The Purge," as well as clown masks.
"I don't think that they were looking for me and my brother. I think they were looking for anybody that they could get stopped at the stop light," Brown said.
The victim also said he had to get staples put in his head and that his brother was stabbed with a machete-like weapon.

-"Victim recognizes teen during brutal attack by 20 people in 'The Purge,' clown masks," *WFTV9 ABC*, last updated November 1, 2016.

Maggie told me the Burger King at the gas station was the only place to eat after 8:00 p.m. I drove a mile north, away from downtown Tonopah, and found a cone of light cast over the parking lot and the pumps. Beyond this circle of warm light lay the perfect, inky blackness of night.

I made some online posts about the Clown Motel. When I posted a photograph of the cemetery, a friend wrote back, *I dare you to walk through there at midnight.*

I replied: *Hahaha. Maybe tomorrow.*

I had been in Tonopah less than 24 hours, and had already collected a handful of ghost stories and firsthand accounts. The waitress who had worked at the Mizpah Hotel, where the deadbolt on the guest's door locked itself from the inside. Her niece, who had taken an audio recording in the graveyard and picked up a voice growling. Jack, who took photos of the clown dolls and found every one twisted and distorted. There had to be something to it.

Sure, superstition exists. Some people do let their imagination run away with them; others are just plain crazy. Not these people, though—everyone I had met so far struck me as rational, level-headed adults. I couldn't believe they were all just making it up. Not to mention, I had heard the footsteps on my ceiling the night before. Nobody told me that one.

Why is it that certain towns—like Tonopah—are a hotbed for strange phenomena? Why do some places seem to hold onto the past?

I walked into the Burger King and took off my heavy jacket. The cashier, a young brunette in her twenties, told me she had grown up in Tonopah. As I chatted with her, I mentioned the piles of discarded metal and glass I had seen during my jog that morning.

"We call that 'the Chinese Junkyard,'" she said. "I think a lot of Chinese mine workers used to live out there, and they dumped their trash there. Just a few blocks from the motel you're staying at, they used to have some kind of Chinese temple and an old jail. I heard there was even a mass grave over there. The Chinese workers who died, they just dumped 'em all in a hole together. Who knows how many people are buried there? No tombstones, no memories. They just covered them up with the *tailings*—the rocks and sand they pulled out of the mine—and forgot about them."

"No wonder this town's haunted," I said.

The cashier turned back toward the kitchen behind her. "Uh... What's that?" She shouted out. "Okay, coming... Excuse me, sir, I've got to go." I hadn't heard anyone call her.

I sat at the corner booth and pulled up some old notes on my phone, from ghost research I had done years ago. The silence inside the Burger King was occasionally broken by the quiet hiss from the air hose outside. I tried to imagine Tonopah during its heyday, a bustling town of thousands of miners.

Mines. Tungsten, gold, and silver. Could the mines have anything to do with the strange phenomena people experienced?

British author Paul Devereux has written a great book, *Haunted Land,* that discusses several theories about why places are haunted. He suggests that certain rocks, such as granite, exist in much higher quantities in haunted places. The minerals in the soil may have a particular kind of magnetism that "records" events of the past, through a process we don't yet understand.

When researching a haunted road near Oxford, Devereux brought some scientists to the area. They detected natural radiation levels three times higher at the "hot spot," where people saw the apparitions, than anywhere else along the road. Could there be something in the soil of an old mining town like Tonopah, I wondered—magnetism, or radiation—that "records" events of the past and keeps them on constant replay?

Devereux also quotes an engineer, Vic Tandy, who researched two haunted buildings in depth: an historic factory and an old home's cellar. Tandy found that low-frequency sound waves, around 19 Hertz cycles per minute, were prevalent in both places. While the sounds could have been caused by natural things of the environment—nearby machinery or the wind—Devereux suggests that certain sound frequencies might have a particular effect on a person's brain.

Of course, a skeptic would call it a hallucination. If sound waves or natural magnetism affect a person's brain, then they're just seeing things that aren't there, right?

There is another possibility, however. What if something is actually there? On a different plane or frequency that we don't normally perceive, sure, but existing nonetheless, out there, all around us. If we "tweak" our brains a little, they might momentarily perceive something that we don't normally see.

If there is some process by which events of the past imprint onto a place, most of them have one thing in common—intense suffering. And old mining towns like Tonopah were no stranger to tragedy. Gunfights, murders, mine accidents. Hundreds of Chinese laborers worked to death and dumped into a hole like animals. Human pain and suffering has a way of imprinting memories on a place, functioning like the flash bulb of a camera.

I liked this theory. In the solitary gas station, surrounded by the vast darkness of the desert, there was something comforting about having a cold, analytical explanation.

Magnetism, metals in the soil, I wrote in my notebook. *Possible recording of the past, natural process. Not so scary.*

That wasn't what I felt, though. I felt that I was approaching some ancient, invisible danger. Something that lurked behind the half-open door of the closet where, as a child, I would stare into the darkness. Something that lay sleeping beneath the earth, that every now and then poked a claw up through the soil of my dreams.

CHAPTER 12
Mister Creepy

"Where there is mystery, it's supposed there must be evil, so we think, 'What are you hiding?'"
  -Dr. Andrew McConnell Stott, professor of the University of Buffalo and clown expert

I stopped into the lobby before heading back to my room. Maggie, the red-haired receptionist, was vacuuming the faded carpet.

"Do you mind if I sit here on the couch and write?" I asked.

"No problem at all. Don't mind me."

She pushed the vacuum under the shelves with the clown dolls. Their faces lit up with the yellow glow from the vacuum's headlight. When she moved underneath the angry, horned clown doll with the handkerchief body, a gust of air puffed the hanky up and the clown jumped, dancing in the air.

The TV was playing the 1968 horror film *Rosemary's Baby*. I recognized the monstrous face and yellow eyes on the screen—this was the scene when the title character was impregnated. *"This is no dream!"* The voice from the TV shouted. *"This is real!"*

As Maggie vacuumed the lobby and the Devil raped Rosemary, I leafed through my notes from that day. The door at the Mizpah Hotel that locked itself... Growling voices on the graveyard recording... The twisted clown faces... Possible effects of metals and magnetism in the earth...

Suddenly, the room was extremely quiet. Maggie had shut off the vacuum and stood leaning against the counter.

"You know," she said, "I heard you and Bill talking." The soft, dramatic music from the movie played in the background. "Bill was right. There is something here."

"Have you… Have you had any experiences here?" I asked.

"I know they're here. I can tell when they're around. Sometimes I get this terrible feeling like… Like I'm not alone."

The music from the movie grew louder and faster.

"How do you handle it?" I asked.

"I try to ignore it most of the time. I just go about my business. I really don't like the voices, though."

"You've heard… Voices? Here, in this motel?"

"I don't like it. It makes me feel… Ugh. Not right."

"Are you sure it isn't just guests from one of the rooms?"

"I wish it was." She leaned forward and lowered her voice. "But no. When you hear them, it's like they're right here in this room with you. Sometimes a man, sometimes a woman. It's always a short phrase, one or two words. And I can never understand what they're saying. It's in a foreign language, I think. You know, back in the mining days, people came here from all over."

A close up of Rosemary's face appeared on the TV, desperation and terror in her eyes.

"But that's… Is it just here in the lobby that strange things happen?"

"In the rooms too." Maggie glanced at the clown dolls on the top shelves. "Just today, the man staying in Room 102 came in to ask me who was in the room above him. 'Somebody was running around up there last night,' he said. Well, I told him that there's nobody staying in that room. In fact, there are no guests in any of the three rooms above 102."

I stared at Maggie. "And he's sure he heard footsteps?"

"That's what I asked him. 'Maybe it was cats on the roof?' No, he said, it definitely couldn't have been cats. It was heavy footsteps, he said. Like a full-grown man running around."

The TV cut to a commercial for a home security system. *Don't gamble on the safety of your loved ones,* the announcer said while, onscreen, a prowler lurked outside a bedroom window.

"The same thing happened to me last night," I whispered softly. "I heard footsteps, too."

"I'm not surprised," Maggie said. "There is something here all right. These clowns, for instance. Some of them have a mind all their own. See that one, down on the floor?" She pointed out a short, squat ceramic statue with real orange hair, behind the large Ronald McDonald mannequin. "You know why I put him back there?"

"Is he on time out?" I joked.

"He moves." She was dead serious. "He used to be out here with the others. But he'd move. He'd be on the shelf when I started vacuuming, and when I turned around, I'd see him clear on the other side of the room."

"He looks so innocent. Now this guy, on the other hand..." I nodded towards the life-sized doll in the rocking chair next to me, with the realistic wooden hands.

"Ugh. I don't like him at all." Maggie folded her arms across her chest. "I call him 'Mister Creepy.'"

"I can see why."

I looked at the glossy, white face, the waxy round cheeks, the smug grin. I turned away and faced the TV. Rosemary had entered the Satanists' lair and found her baby. *"What have you done to it?"* she screamed in horror. *"What have you done to its eyes?"* The male Satanist answered, *"He has his father's eyes."*

"I've seen his hand move before," Maggie said, still staring at Mister Creepy. "When I'm in here by myself. I'll be standing here behind the counter, minding my own business, and I look up, and I see that wooden hand slide across his leg."

The dialogue from the TV continued in the background.

"What are you talking about?! Guy's eyes are normal! What have you done to him, you maniacs?!"

"Satan is his father, not Guy! He came up from Hell and begat a son of mortal woman."

"We had a woman stay here a while ago who was a professional psychic," Maggie said. "She told me that things happen here because we are so close to the graveyard. Like whatever is over there, it creeps over here and gets into the motel."

"Hail Adrian!" cried the voices of the Satanists from the TV. *"Hail Satan!"*

"And she got a terrible feeling from Mister Creepy," Maggie said. "She didn't want to touch him or even go near him."

"No! It can't be!" Rosemary screamed. A female Satanist countered, *"Look at his hands, his feet!"*

"What did the psychic say about Mr. Creepy?" I whispered, glancing at the wooden hands next to me.

"She said that she felt like there was… Something inside the doll. Something living inside him."

CHAPTER 13
The Hissing

Winchester Police are investigating after a report of a woman being assaulted by a man in a clown mask. Police say she was walking on a trail Friday night when she says a man in a clown mask attacked her and tried to drag her into the woods.
   -"Police investigating report of a woman attacked by man in clown mask in Winchester, Kentucky," *WDRB News,* published October 1, 2016.

Maggie locked up the lobby and I headed up to my room. I tried the TV again. Still nothing but fuzz. I hit the knob to turn it off, and the amorphous "ghost" of colored light appeared on the screen for a second.

I thought I'd cheer myself up by watching watch some *Key and Peele* comedy sketches. I turned on my laptop—no WiFi signal. My phone wasn't getting any connection, either. I laid down on the bed and read a chapter of Stephen King's *IT*.

The silence was punctuated by the occasional creaks and groans of the motel. The entire building seemed to be breathing.

Around midnight, I put the book down and went to bed. After tossing and turning for far too long, I finally drifted off to sleep.

A loud creak woke me back up. My room was bathed in the soft yellow light filtered through the worn curtains. I turned towards the window.

A silhouette stood outside. Facing my room, legs at a wide stance, arms hanging at his sides. He stared in, as if he could see me.

I held my breath. *Should I call the reception desk? But they close at night...*

He cocked his head to one side.

Should I call the cops?

As I gaped at the window in horror, the figure slowly turned to the right.

Oh shit oh shit oh shit.

He was wearing a clown nose. It stuck far out from his profile, round and bulbous. The curly wig hung off the back of his skull. His long, oversized sleeves puffed out around the wrists. It was a clown.

He turned back towards me. He stared inward. And he started hissing. God help me, the clown was hissing like a snake.

SsssssssSSSsssssSSSsssss...

The air came out long and steady, no breaks. A steady, outward stream of air blown through his teeth, on and on, never taking a breath.

He leaned forward and banged his forehead against the window. *TAP.* He brought it back and forward again. *TAP.* Over and over. *TAP. TAP. TAP.*

My heart was in my throat. I tried to scream. I couldn't. The clown banged his head against the glass, hissing even louder.

"HELP!"

When I finally got the word out, I sat bolt upright. I opened my eyes and turned to the window. No silhouette, no clown. Nothing but the yellow light from the outdoor bulb.

It had all been a dream. The red numbers on the nightstand clock read 2:27 a.m. I could still hear the hissing. I rubbed my eyes and slapped my own cheeks to make sure I was fully awake. *It can't be...*

The tapping sound continued as well.

Is this a dream within a dream?

The hissing came from somewhere outside my door.

Okay, now I actually am going to call someone.

I checked my phone. No reception. Still, the hissing and the tapping continued, slow and rhythmic, like voiceless, otherworldly music.

I wanted to go check, but I was too terrified to get out of bed. The conventional wisdom of childhood had never felt more real: *The monsters can't get me as long as I stay under the covers. Or the clowns. If I set one foot on the floor, they can grab me with their clawed, white-gloved hands. Blankets are impenetrable to monsters, though. Just stay put.*

The hissing continued. I tried calling the motel's number that was saved on my phone. Still no service. I reached over and grabbed my laptop off the nightstand. No WiFi. No way of contacting anyone.

I'll take a video. I can record it and save it on my laptop. Then if a clown kills me, at least there will be evidence of my murder for the Forensic Team to find. And maybe some of my books will go up in value.

I opened a video program on my laptop, hit the *record* button, and started talking to the glowing eye of the camera. It felt ridiculous. *I'm alone in a motel room, talking to a computer about how I'm feeling. What am I, a millennial?*

A strange thing happened, though, as I held the computer in one hand and described the strange sounds around me—I did feel less alone. Sure, these might be my last words—some killer clown might break into my room, and my unseen viewers would be the only witnesses to my grizzly murder—but someone would hear me. I even mustered the courage to get out of bed.

I walked around the room and discussed the sounds: the creaking from the ceiling; the rhythmic *tap, tap, tap*; the hissing. I spoke in a hushed voice, my face glowing faint blue in the light of the screen. I half wished that I could conjure some snot from my nose, to really give it that *Blair Witch Project* flair.

I traced the tapping to the bathroom. When I got a light on it, I realized that the shower head was leaking. What had sounded like a psychotic clown banging his head against the window was nothing more than a dripping faucet.

The more I talked to the camera, the more I penetrated the veil of solitude. I felt gradually braver. The hissing continued, and I was going to get to the bottom of it. I traced the source to somewhere near the door. I walked closer, feeling the folds in the carpet with my bare feet to keep from tripping.

Whether some desert snake was trying to slither into my room, or whether a murderous clown crouching hissing at my window, I needed to know the truth. I pressed my ear to the door. It was coming from somewhere outside.

Here goes nothing...

I pulled the latch chain off and unlocked the door knob. "Let's see what's out there," I whispered to the laptop camera.

The door creaked open. A gust of freezing air blew in. I peeked around the edge, slowly. The faded blue Astroturf of the walkway was empty. I peered around to the right. The hissing was insanely loud, coming from the other side of the street. I stepped one bare foot out of the room, holding the laptop in my left hand, and took a look.

A car wash.

Across the highway from the motel, a self-serve car wash glowed in the darkness. Two booths had been equipped with hoses and automatic soap dispensers. For reasons unknown, somebody had decided to wash his car at three in the morning. As Rick James once observed, cocaine is a hell of a drug.

I saved the video to my computer and shut it off. When I laid back down on the bed, my mind was at ease. My eyes grew heavy. My muscles relaxed.

Before I drifted off to sleep, however, one nagging thought tugged at my mind:

THREE NIGHTS IN THE CLOWN MOTEL

Still, I'm certain I heard those footsteps on the ceiling last night. And I've got no logical explanation for that one.

CHAPTER 14
The Moving Hand

"Very few children like clowns. They are unfamiliar and come from a different era. They don't look funny, they just look odd."
    -Patricia Doorbar, British child psychologist

I headed down to the lobby for some stale coffee the next morning. My eyes felt crusty and dry. Multiple nights of sleep deprivation had left me with a surreal sense of detachment. I was approaching the "Fight Club" level of insomnia, where everything was a copy of a copy of a copy.

The bells on the lobby door jangled as I entered. The enormous Ronald McDonald statue stood at the entrance, one hand frozen in a wave. I waved back. His eyes stared into space. They reminded me of a teacher I had in Junior High, who always showed the whites around his pupils. "Crazy eyes," my parents said after they met him at Back to School Night.

"Hello, I don't think we've met yet," I told the receptionist. She was in her forties, with wavy blonde hair and a friendly smile.

"Pleased to meet you. I'm Brandi."

I poured myself some coffee and took a couple photos of the clowns dangling from the ceiling. The sunlight shone brightly through the window. The lobby felt warm and cozy in the morning light, after that first sip of coffee. Even Mister Creepy, despite his veiny wooden hands and his grim smile, looked less threatening.

"So what brought you to Tonopah?" Brandi asked.

"Clowns and ghosts," I said.

"You're not the only one," she chuckled. "I guess a lot of stuff has been getting around the internet lately. We get more and more prank phone calls every day. People call up and say weird things, or talk in a silly clown voice, or make jokes. We're pretty sick of it by now, to tell the truth." She glanced down at the rotary phone and puffed air out through her teeth. "And they won't shut up about the ham story."

"Ham?"

"Some kids made it up," she said. "They wrote it in an online review. Said they were staying here and they heard a weird noise behind their bathroom window. They looked out the window and saw somebody…"

"Yes?"

"It's so dumb. They say they saw someone dressed like a clown, having sex with a ham."

"I can see how that would be made up," I laughed. "For one thing, the bathrooms on this motel don't even have windows."

"And another thing," Brandi said, "people here aren't perverts. I can assure you, nobody has sex with ham in Tonopah."

"I'll take your word for it." She laughed. "But I guess any publicity is good publicity, right? Didn't they film a TV show here? With the ghost hunters?"

"Oh yeah, *Ghost Adventures*," she said. "I was working here at the time. I saw them set the whole thing up."

"Set what up?" I asked, intrigued.

"The scene where that guy's hand moves." She pointed at Mister Creepy. "They staged it. I came in here when they were tying the fishing line to his hand."

"Well good to know he's not *too* possessed. I keep thinking I'm going to see him standing by my bed at night."

"No, it was staged," she grinned. "And I'm glad to know it was. I work in here alone sometimes. The second that thing actually moves on its own, I'm getting the hell out of here!"

"I don't blame you!" I didn't mention that Maggie had told me she had seen Mister Creepy's hand move when no camera crews were around.

"Also," Brandi continued, "they had a scene on that ghost show where the door opened by itself. I remember, we had just replaced the knob at the time, and it wouldn't latch right. And you've seen the strong winds we get out here."

"Just the wind. Makes sense."

The ghosts and unknown terrors in my mind were fading fast. With every fresh ray of sunlight that broke in, every new drop of caffeine coursing through my veins, the rational part of my brain grew stronger. Life was making sense again.

The phone rang and Brandi answered it. I went to top off my cup of coffee. After she hung up, I asked, "Another crank caller? Asking about the ham?"

"No, thank God," she said. "There's all kinds of nuts out there. One thing I can tell you was genuine, though, when the *Ghost Adventures* guys were here: when they went into the graveyard."

A cloud passed over the sun, casting the lobby in shadow. Brandi gave a glance over her shoulder.

"They took all their equipment into the cemetery, to film at night. They had just charged their batteries. And all the batteries drained as soon as they walked into the graveyard. Every single one."

"Are you sure it wasn't the power source here at the motel?"

"No, because they had brought three different generators with them. All three of them died at the same time. And they're not the only ones; it happens here all the time. The poor maintenance guy who helps us out, he's always dealing with it. The batteries will be brand new in a remote, and they'll drain right away. The different appliances here stop working, then come back on a minute later.

"When you live here long enough, eventually you just get used to that sort of thing. It happens everywhere in Tonopah."

"Maggie was telling me a few stories last night." I glanced at Mister Creepy. "About a psychic who came here…"

"A man?" Brandi asked.

"No, she said it was a female psychic. Why, did a male psychic stay here, too?" I could imagine this place would be a popular spot for anyone connected to the paranormal.

"The guy I met was a man in his fifties," Brandi said. "He told us he had a gift. That he was a 'sensitive.' He came in when Maggie was working here behind the desk. He told her he saw the figure of a woman standing behind her. She freaked out and left early that day."

"Do you think maybe he was just messing with her?" I asked, playing the skeptical devil's advocate.

"I don't know, but I met him the next day. He said he was going to go into the cemetery. He wanted to see if he could 'sense' anything in there."

"What did he find?" I asked.

"I don't know. He never came back to tell us what he found. Left like he was in a hurry to get out of here. Didn't even come in to say goodbye."

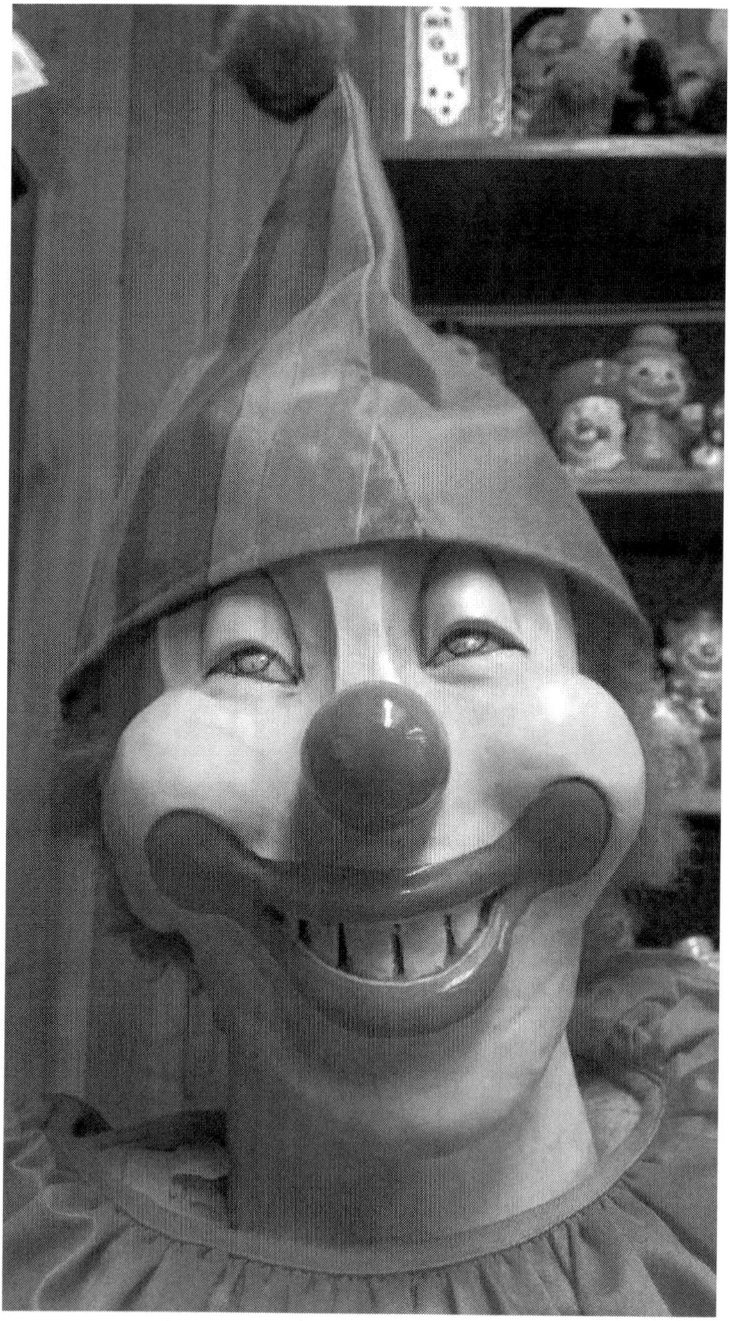

CHAPTER 15

"Don't Tempt Fate"

Around 4 a.m. Friday, a woman smoking on her porch claimed a man dressed in a striped outfit, a red wig and a white clown mask grabbed her around the throat. The victim told police that the clown immediately said, "I should just kill you now" and that some students and teachers would wish they were never born at the junior and senior high school today.

-T.J. Parker and Rose-Ann Aragon, "Clown attack forces several schools in Ohio to cancel Friday's classes," *WCPO*, published September 29, 2016.

The coffee and the chat with Brandi had me feeling positive. When I checked my email and saw a message from an editor interested in publishing one of my books, my mood improved even more. Even the clown painting on the wall felt less menacing.

I locked my room and drove across town to have breakfast at the diner again. Under the blue, cloudless sky, Main Street felt downright cheery. I noticed a bookstore with the front door open. A handful of people were walking around. If my life were a movie, this would be the scene with *Bright, Sunshiney Day* playing in the background.

Just one more night here. No big deal, I said to myself. *I can handle one more night. No sweat.*

I thought of the novella *Viy* by Russian author Nikolai Gogol. The main character is a seminary student, plagued by doubt and insecurity, who is commissioned to pray over the body of a dead girl. The girl has been accused of witchcraft. The villagers lock him inside an old, abandoned church with the corpse, which comes to life and terrorizes him.

On the third day, he begins to feel hopeful. "By tomorrow," he says, "I'll be free of this torment. I just need to make it through one more night."

It's true, I thought. *One more night in a haunted place isn't so bad.*

Then I remembered how the *Viy* story ends: on that third night, he dies of fright.

I wasn't being locked up with a witch's corpse, though. I just had to make it through one more night in a remote Clown Motel. I could spend this last day collecting stories. I wanted to get some good videos and photos as well. I had already recorded my room and the clown infestation in the motel lobby. What else could I film? The "Chinese junkyard" on the outskirts of town offered a nice, apocalyptic scene. The boarded up storefronts on Main Street looked desolate and haunted. The red-brick Mizpah Hotel might be nice. Or…

The graveyard.

Nearly all the stories pointed back to the graveyard. The locals all described it in similar terms: the clowns were creepy, but the graveyard was what caused the phenomena. The ghosts drifted over to the motel, like radiation or pollen. If a haunting had an "epicenter," the graveyard was it.

I remembered the message my friend posted the night before: *I dare you to walk through there at night.* What if I took him up on his dare?

I have always been a sucker for peer pressure. I remember reading a story in Alvin Schwartz's *Scary Stories to Tell in the Dark,* about a girl whose friends dare her to walk across a graveyard and stick a knife in the ground as proof. The story always made me anxious. I knew that if my friends ever challenged me in that way, I wouldn't be able to turn them down. Maybe it's macho bravado, maybe it's a matter of caring too much what others think. Like Marty McFly, "Nobody calls me chicken" has long been my mantra.

It would make for a great video. Bring in some new readers for my work, expand my fan base. I could handle a little walk through the graveyard, right?

I could always broadcast a live video on Facebook. I would keep the camera going the entire time. I wouldn't be "alone" in the strictest sense—friends and relatives would be watching me in real time. I would carry hundreds of people in the palm of my hand, a constant stream of hearts and happy face emoticons flowing across the screen, reacting to my video.

I recalled the previous night: as soon as I started recording, I felt less isolated. As long as I was connected to the outside world, the eerie sounds of the motel were manageable.

Of course, if a corpse did reach its hand up from the cold earth and grab my ankle, there wouldn't be much that my friends could do about it. 300 miles away was still 300 miles away. At least they would have recorded evidence of what happened to me. Added bonus—if I was dragged into the underworld on live video, my books would definitely increase in value.

By the time I took my seat at the diner counter, my mind was made up. I posted on every social media site:

> *Stay tuned. Going to walk across the graveyard at midnight. Will broadcast live. (Forgive the pun.)*

I wasn't going to mention my plans to the motel staff. The graveyard had no hours or time limits posted, so it couldn't be *that* illegal. Still, it's always easier to ask for forgiveness than ask for permission.

The younger, brunette waitress with the French braid poured me a cup of coffee. She appeared to be working alone that morning. After she took my order, I checked my phone. Several people had already reacted to my post, mostly with the "surprised face" emoticon. One friend texted me: *This graveyard you're walking through... Is it, like, a clown graveyard?*

When I clarified that it was just an ordinary cemetery that happened to be next door to the Clown Motel, he replied:

Oh, good. I was imagining a clown grave with a little hand crank next it. When you turn the crank, a music box plays Pop Goes the Weasel. *And guess what pops out when the song gets to the end...*

I replied: *I'll make a note to recommend that to the Tonopah Board of Tourism.*

I put my phone away and pulled out Stephen King's *IT*. I had come to the part where Beverly is in the bathroom and hears a voice inside the drain. *"You'll float down here, Beverly,"* it tells her from deep in the sewer. *"We all float down here..."* The voice drifts away, choking and hiccupping, and a bubble of blood expands from the sink's drain and pops.

"That's fucked up," a voice behind me said. I turned.

A group of bikers, all muscles and beards and bellies and tattoos, sat at a long table. The French braid waitress was telling them about the motel.

"That's right," she said, "the lobby's full of hundreds of clown dolls. So if you don't like clowns..."

"I've never liked clowns," said a red-haired woman in a leather vest.

"I always thought they were creepy," a burly man with a bushy moustache said. "Not a big fan."

"That's not all," the waitress said, "the motel's right next door to an old cemetery."

"No thanks!" the biker said, exhaling like he'd been punched in the stomach. "I'll skip that one!"

When the waitress came to refill my coffee, I told her I was staying there.

"I used to live nearby 'The Clown,'" she said, "in the trailer park behind it."

"Wow. What do you think about all the ghost stories people tell about the place?"

"Well, I never experienced anything there myself. Then again, I never stayed in the motel. I had a friend who used to work there, though. Briefly."

"Briefly?" I asked.

"She only lasted a week." The waitress looked behind her, as if telling a secret. "My friend was making up the beds in the rooms one day. Another woman who worked there was training her. All of a sudden, my friend felt a hand brush across her ear and cheek. 'Hey,' she said to the other woman, 'did you touch me?' 'Of course I didn't touch you,' the woman said. 'I'm clear over here, on the other side of the room.' Well my friend got the heck out of there. Never went back."

The waitress went for my food. The bikers behind me laughed at a dirty joke.

"When I lived over there," the waitress said when she returned, "by 'The Clown,' lots of my friends and relatives refused to even visit me. They'd heard too many stories. In a small town like this, word gets around fast."

She checked on the bikers' table, and I checked on my phone. I wanted to make sure my Facebook app was working, and I would be able to broadcast live video. When I tried searching for the "go live" function, though, a message appeared: *YOUR FACEBOOK APP NEEDS TO BE UPDATED.* I tried downloading the new version. *INSUFFICIENT SPACE ON YOUR PHONE TO DOWNLOAD THIS APP,* it said.

I stared at the screen. *If I can't stream a live video, do I still want to go through with this?*

The phone vibrated with an incoming call, from my girlfriend Carlita.

"Hey *Carlita Chula,*" I said, "how's it going?"

"Don't do it," she replied. Her voice was dead serious. "I just saw your post about walking through the cemetery tonight. I don't want you to do it. I dreamed about you last night."

"What happened in your dream?" I asked, intrigued.

"It—it was bad. I couldn't sleep all night."

"You don't need to worry about me, Carlita," I said. "I'm just going to take a little video. It'll be good publicity for my books."

"But what if something happens to you?" Her voice shook slightly.

"Nothing's going to happen to me. Those people are all dead."

"I mean something… Supernatural. You know."

"Look, I'm not going to tell you that spirits or demons straight up don't exist," I said. "But if they do, I don't think they can just pop up and 'get' you. I mean, I'm not holding a séance or anything. It's not like I'm going to tempt fate…"

"David. You're walking across a *graveyard*. At *midnight*. You don't think that's the definition of 'tempting fate'?"

"I'm sure I'll be fine." I sounded less confident than I intended.

"Just think about what you're doing, David," she said. "You know what they say: *Si la buscas, la encuentras.* If you go looking for the supernatural, you just might find it."

CHAPTER 16

"They Are Still Here"

Shawn Freemore and Ian Seagraves remained expressionless Wednesday as a jury convicted them of first-degree murder in the February 2009 fatal stabbing of Michael Goucher in Price Township. [...] Both defendants call themselves Juggalos, *a subculture with some members carrying butcher knives and meat cleavers and listening to violent "horror-core" rock/rap songs from groups such as* Insane Clown Posse *and* Twiztid.

-Andrew Scott, "Cresco men guilty in Juggalo murder trial," *Pocono Record,* published September 22, 2011.

I stopped by the bookstore on Main Street on my way back to the motel. It was one of those good, old-fashioned *Beauty and the Beast* kind of shops: stacks of mismatched, used books, their covers faded into a collage of muted pastels. The air smelled of old paper and dust. The shelves were so close together, you had to slide in between them sideways. A handful of books covered the history of Tonopah, with some legends and ghost stories from Nevada's mining country. As I leafed through an old copy of Steinbeck's *Travels with Charley in Search of America,* a fresh text message vibrated its way into my pocket. *I'll just bet that's somebody writing to warn me,* I thought, *saying it's not a good idea to walk through a haunted graveyard at midnight.*

Sure enough, the message began:

Hey, David. I'm not trying to tell you what to do, but... Are you sure this is a good idea?

I checked my phone's storage again. There was no way I would be able to download the update for the Facebook app, which

I would need to broadcast live from the cemetery. I could always record a video with my phone's camera, though, and upload it to YouTube later on.

Did I want to do that, though?

I imagined being out there alone, at midnight. Broadcasting a live video would have felt like a lifeline to the outside world. But *recording* a video? That was more like sticking a message into a bottle and tossing it out to sea, hoping somebody might read it someday.

The idea of going out there was no longer just a publicity stunt. It had become a personal challenge, a test to myself, to see if I could actually face these old fears.

Psychologists talk about a principle called "mastery," when we deal with what we fear by facing it head-on. Spending three nights alone in the Clown Motel was a challenge in and of itself. I felt like I was blazing through five years worth of therapy in one weekend. My mind drifted back to that day at Disneyland when I was five, the leering clowns' faces, the figure behind the tombstone. Walking across the Tonopah graveyard at midnight would be the ultimate test.

"Can I help you find something?" the blonde, twenty-something girl behind the counter asked me.

"Oh, I was just looking at these ghost books." I picked one up from the front window and mentioned my mission to explore the Clown Motel.

"I used to work there!" She said.

"No kidding? You don't happen to be friends with a waitress at the diner down the street, do you?" I told her the story about the girl who felt a hand brush her face in the motel.

"No, that wasn't me, thank God. But I definitely felt like I wasn't alone. You can feel them. They come over from the graveyard. You can tell when they're around."

I offered to donate a copy of my book *Holy Ghosts* to the bookstore.

"That's so nice of you!" she said. "Another ghost book for the collection. Let me go get Larry; he's the owner."

A minute later, a gray-haired man with glasses greeted me. I handed him my book and told him about my research at the Clown Motel.

"There's something about that place, all right." He spoke with a steady, soft tone, friendly but serious. "It's like a magnet for strange things. The first time I set foot in there, I saw a painting hanging in the lobby that looked incredibly familiar. I thought for a minute, and realized that I had seen it as a kid, at my grandma's house. She lived hundreds of miles away. Never came to Nevada in her life. But there was the painting—a one-of-a-kind original—hanging in 'The Clown.'"

"That's so bizarre."

"I mean, I'm sure it has a logical explanation. It must have gotten sold at a garage sale somewhere, and found its way up here. Still, there's something about this whole town. This valley, these hills… The land holds onto the past. Even here, in this bookstore."

The phone rang and he answered it. I flipped through a couple of the books on the counter.

"One of 'them' is right here, in this bookstore," Larry continued after hanging up. "A spirit, if you want to call it that. I think it might be a friend of mine. He used to come in here every day and help me make coffee. One morning he walked in, keeled over, and died. Right there where you're standing, by that aisle."

I looked at the ground, half expecting to see a blood stain.

"I feel like he's still here," Larry said. "We hear strange noises. Books fly off the shelves. You can ask anyone who works here."

He thanked me for the copy of *Holy Ghosts* and let me take the Steinbeck book for free.

"There's a lot of history here, all right," he said as we bid goodbye. "The mining days, the Old West. That graveyard by 'The Clown.' They never left. They are still here. If you spend enough time in this town, you're bound to experience something."

CHAPTER 17
"It Followed Her Home"

La commedia è finita!
 -Pagliacci the Clown, after murdering his wife and her lover

The sky had clouded over by the time I left the bookstore. Drizzle beaded up on my windshield. As I drove back to the motel in the waning sunlight, I was having serious second thoughts about walking through the graveyard that night.

In the morning, I had felt confident about this publicity stunt. It would be a cake walk. As the day went on, it became a personal challenge, a chance to face my fears. Then I talked to the waitress, and my girlfriend, and the bookstore employee, and Larry. They were all on the same wavelength. By sunset, a new sensation was creeping in—the real possibility that, if I went out there, something might actually happen to me.

The thick, viscous dread spreading across my stomach sent me back in time. The brown desert of Tonopah and the low-lying black clouds faded away, and I was back at Round Table Pizza in northern California. The year was 1993.

Sunshine streamed in through the faux Medieval stained glass windows. My parents had ordered my favorite pizza, but I couldn't eat it. There was no way I could enjoy the food or the video games when I knew what lay ahead: in minutes, I would board the bus for Sixth Grade Camp.

That night, I would sleep in a cold, drafty cabin in the woods. Away from home for the first time in my life. Every second that ticked away on the clock brought me closer to communal showers and dark, fetid outhouses. Nothing but a pimply teenage counselor would stand between me and the camp bullies.

I could have backed out, of course. Nobody forced me onto that bus. I could always back out now, too. I had told thousands of online readers that I would do it, but I could always make something up for them. Invent a flash flood, a police raid of the Clown Motel, something that prevented me from going through with it. If I did chicken out, though—now, as in Sixth Grade—I knew I would never forgive myself.

Still, the dread grew. I just wanted to jump ahead in time, to suddenly lose consciousness and wake up at some lovely future moment when it would all be behind me.

Eager for a distraction, I parked and went into the motel lobby for a candy bar. Brandi, the blonde woman I had met that morning, was just finishing her shift. I gave her a $5 bill and she headed to the back room for change.

I noticed, for the first time, a plush doll sitting on "Mr. Creepy's" lap. Its hair was made of crude yellow yarn, arranged in a symmetrical "bowl cut." The eyes were two black buttons, expressionless and soulless. A thin line of black thread formed the mouth. The abstract face didn't smile—it *gaped.* I recalled the story of "Harold" from Alvin Schwartz's *Scary Stories to Tell in the Dark,* about a scarecrow that comes to life. This clown's featureless face rivaled that of Harold. It was a *tabula rasa* on which to write evil, the kind of face you could easily imagine it coming to life.

The bells on the door jingled and Jack came in, wearing the same denim jacket and baseball cap. He plopped down on the couch.

"Hey there, David."

"Hello again." I leaned against the counter. "Any more weird clown photos show up on your phone?"

He chuckled. "No, it's working fine for now. But I just remembered something. You're writing ghost stories, right?"

"That's right."

"Well, I thought you might like to hear about something... Something I saw."

The TV continued to broadcast news about the shooter on the Vegas Strip.

"I went out for a walk last night, to buy some smokes from the gas station. As I was coming back, I looked over at the graveyard and noticed a bright light. Just hovering in the air, right above the tombstones. At first, thought it was a helicopter. But it didn't move. It just hung there for a long time."

I stared at the shelf above his head. A clown with black hair and a pasty white face stared back at me. Its only features were a couple of small, black eyes and a tiny wisp of a mouth. It could have been one of the "greys" that people describe in alien abduction stories.

"When I got closer," Jack continued, "I saw that the light wasn't up in the sky somewhere. It was close up, hovering right above the gravestones. Then it started to move, slowly. It got lower, and lower, and it split in two. The lights went flying off away from each other, and sunk into the ground."

"There's something here, all right." Brandi came back with my change and my candy bar. Her eyes smiled, but her face was uncharacteristically serious. "You work here long enough, it can't be ignored."

"Room 108, that's the really haunted one, isn't it?" The man asked.

"It's one of them," Brandi responded. "I didn't believe Maggie when she told me, back when I was new here. Then one day, I was changing the sheets in 108. The door was shut, and I had my back to it. When I turned around to grab the pillowcases, I screamed. The table and chair had moved right in front of the door. Nobody else was even on shift that day."

"I don't think we'll be telling my wife that one," Jack said with a wry smile. "She doesn't need any more reasons to be scared of this place."

"Did *you* ever see lights in the cemetery?" I asked Brandi.

"Not lights. But I know there's something there. We had a guest who stayed for about a week once. She was like you. Came here looking for ghosts. On her last night here, she went into the graveyard at night to take pictures. 'I want to do some ghost photography,' she said. She came in the next morning and showed me the photos on the camera. She seemed disappointed—she hadn't gotten any 'orbs,' those little balls of light that some people say are spirits."

The sky outside was nearly black. The interior of the lobby reflected off the windows, rows and rows of clown faces staring at us.

"The girl checked out that same day, and we said our goodbyes. A couple weeks later, though, she called me up. Said she needed to talk to someone. When she uploaded the pictures to her computer, a bunch of orbs showed up. 'Sounds like you got some spirit photographs after all,' I told her. That's not all I got,' she said. Her voice sounded shaky. 'Ever since I went into the cemetery that night, I think something... Followed me home.'"

The TV went blank and silent, a minute of dead air before the next commercial came on.

"After that girl got back home," Brandi continued, "she felt like she wasn't alone. Appliances in her house would turn on by themselves. Her microwave, the lights. Her hair dryer, when she was in the bath. It got worse and worse. She felt something jumping on her bed at night, making her mattress shake. She started crying on the phone when she told me. 'Something followed me home,' she kept repeating, 'something followed me home.'"

THREE NIGHTS IN THE CLOWN MOTEL

I told her I would pray for her, and not to worry too much. I didn't tell her what I was really thinking—if you go looking for spirits, you can't be surprised if you find them.

CHAPTER 18
Solitude

Chief Inspector Paul Staniforth said: "We've now received 18 reports of people dressed up as clowns throughout Gwent. Some of the reports have included clowns running through gardens and peering through windows, lurking around shopping centres, parks and schools and jumping from trees."

-Huw Silk, "Clowns 'running through gardens and peering through windows' according to police," *Wales Online,* last updated October 10, 2016.

I checked the time—three hours to midnight. A surge of Sixth Grade Camp dread swelled in my gut. I went for a walk down Main Street to clear my head. It was cold, windy, and empty. I decided to have dinner at the Mizpah, the historic hotel downtown, hoping that a hot meal would put me in a better mood.

The Mizpah was ornately decorated, a well-preserved relic from the early twentieth century. Every wood surface shone, every lamp glowed brightly. A fleeting thought crossed my mind—what if I just bailed on the whole Clown Motel mission?

A skinny boy in a bowtie stood behind the desk. His nametag said *Jonah.*

"Just out of curiosity," I said, "how much does a room here cost, Jonah?"

"The ones we have available right now are $180," he said. Four times as much as my room at the Clown Motel. Far beyond my budget.

The ornate lobby was entirely empty. The wide wooden beams of the high ceilings, the thick carpet, the designs carved in the woodwork, all promised comfort, opulence, and safety. *Just get a room here,* the dark red carpet seemed to whisper in a soothing British accent. *There are no clowns here, no graveyards. You can slip into a warm bath and forget the whole thing. It will be so easy...* A back hallway led to a locked door with a darkened bar behind it. It looked nearly identical to the bar from *The Shining.*

I had given up alcohol for Lent, as I do every year. I was as dry as Jack Nicholson's character in the movie. And never had I wanted a drink more badly.

At the opposite end of the hotel, in the casino, two solitary men sat at the bar playing video poker.

"Do you serve food here?" I asked the bartender.

"Just well drinks." He shook a half-empty bottle of Jim Beam. I thanked him and moved on to the hotel's food court. It was closed. I went back to the casino.

"Is there any place to eat around here?" I asked the bartender.

"At this hour, just the gas station next door."

So much for a hot meal.

I bought a bag of pretzels at the gas station and stood eating them on the cold street corner. A light glowed in a window across the street. A saloon. It looked open.

If I can't have a hot meal and I can't have a drink, I can at least enjoy some human company. I pocketed the pretzels and walked over.

The Country-Western song *She Thinks My Tractor's Sexy* played on the jukebox when I walked in. A couple of locals leaned stoically against the bar, drinking in silence. Two middle-aged men played pool in the back. One of them, wearing a CAT trucker cap, staggered slightly whenever he lined up his shot.

"Haven't seen you in here before." A broad-shouldered blonde in her thirties was working behind the bar.

"Just in town for a few days," I said. "I'm staying at the Clown Motel."

"Oh yeah, there was another guy who came through here a while ago!" She said. "He lived there for, like, a month. He would come in here all the time."

"Chris Sebela, right?" I said. "I just read some of his Tweets."

The man in the trucker cap staggered over to the other end of the bar. He stared at the empty space in front of him, trying to order a drink from someone only he could see. The bartender waved him away dismissively.

"Yeah," she said to me, "Chris was writing about 'The Clown' when he was here. You a writer, too?"

"Yep. I'm collecting stories. Going to walk through the cemetery tonight."

"Whoa," she said, "Chris never did anything that insane!"

As if on cue, Patsy Cline's *Crazy* started playing on the jukebox.

"Yeah…" I muttered. "I'm going to take a video and post it online. If I survive." I managed a meek laugh.

"Now I know why you're in here. Getting some liquid courage before you go out there?" She moved towards the bottles of liquor.

"I wish… But I gave it up Lent. I'll just take a club soda with lime."

"Holy shit. You *are* insane."

She slid my virgin drink across the counter. The man in the trucker cap waved her over. When she replied, "You're cut off, Rick," he laid down on the floor, pulled his cap over his face, and took a little nap.

Three young people, two men and a woman, sat at the opposite corner of the bar. Definitely out-of-towners, their speech lacked any hint of the "desert accent." When I asked, they said they were visiting from northern Nevada, passing through Tonopah on their way to Vegas.

"I overheard you talking about that Clown Motel," the girl said. She wore thick-framed hipster glasses and had her hair cropped short. "Have you been inside that place?"

"I'm staying there," I said.

"Wow. Why? It looks incredibly creepy."

"Supposed to be haunted," I said. "I'm looking for the ghosts."

"I don't believe in such things, personally." She spoke with unusual precision. I pegged her as someone fresh out of college, at that point in life when you still know everything about the world. In a strange way, I missed those days. "I do believe in energy, however."

"So you don't think there's such a thing as a haunted house?" I asked.

"Certainly not."

"You seem pretty sure of that."

"Absolutely."

"Want to go with me tonight when I walk through the graveyard, then?"

"No way in hell."

She turned back to her friends.

The jukebox came back on, playing *The Devil Went down to Georgia*. I checked the clock: It was 11:15 p.m. Just enough time to get back and post one more message online before midnight.

"You sure you don't want anything stronger than club soda?" the bartender asked.

I hesitated. The bottles looked terribly inviting.

"Yeah... I'm sure." I put a five dollar bill on the counter and stood up.

"Well, good luck walking through the graveyard," she said. "I'd tell you not to do it, but... Well, I ain't your momma."

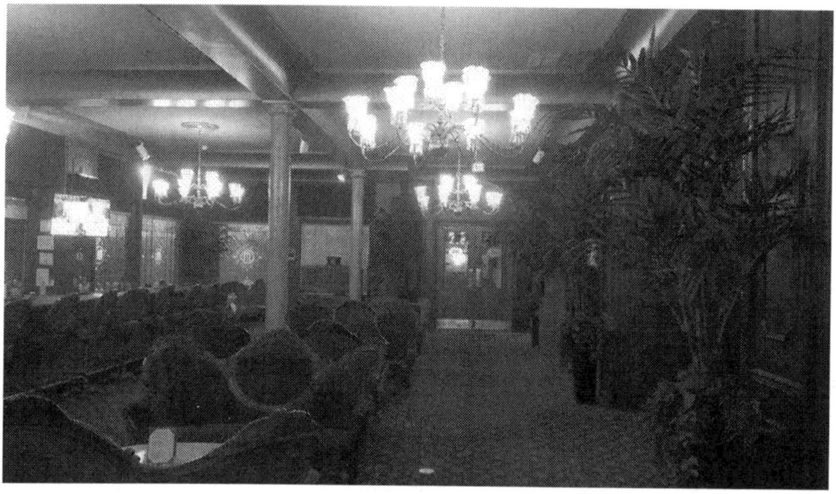

CHAPTER 19
Dread

The wakeful night moved all his fears onto a new level. He was, of course, a materialist in theory; and (also in theory) he was past the age at which one can have night fears. But now, as the wind rattled his window hour after hour, he felt those old terrors again: the old exquisite thrill, as of cold fingers delicately travelling down his back. Materialism is in fact no protection. Those who seek it in that hope (they are not a negligible class) will be disappointed. The thing you fear is impossible. Well and good. Can you therefore cease to fear it? Not here and now. And what then? If you must see ghosts, it is better not to disbelieve in them.
   -C. S. Lewis, *That Hideous Strength*

I walked along the gravelly edge of the highway, back to the motel. The wind kicked up dust devils that glowed in the light of the distant street lamps. It howled. Bushes of roadside chaparral trembled in its wake. I pulled my hat down tighter and dug my hands deep into my pockets.

In a few minutes, I would be walking through the graveyard. I was terrified.

It's amazing how many different states a person's mind can occupy in a single 24-hour period. Earlier this morning, walking through an old cemetery had sounded like the easiest thing in the world. I would do it as a publicity stunt, post a video online, and get a few more readers.

As I heard more stories throughout the day of what happened in the graveyard, I grew more apprehensive. Walking through at night became a personal challenge, a chance to overcome my fears.

Facing your fears is fairly easy, when you know there's nothing that can actually hurt you. It's the same as tackling a "ropes course" with your harness securely fastened, or having your dad throw you into the pool with your floaties on.

The fear mutated as the sun went down, though. By evening, I believed something might *actually* happen to me. And by the time I was walking back from the saloon, the feeling had only strengthened.

I had moved past cocky skepticism, past an openness to the *possibility* of the paranormal. By this point, I *knew* there was something out there. Something with an independent, objective existence that didn't depend on my belief in it. Something I shouldn't be messing with. Something real.

The lobby was already dark when I got back. Maggie stood under the halogen light of the parking lot, hugging herself to stay warm.

"Waiting for your ride?" I asked.

"Oh yeah, I always get a ride home," she said, tucking her chin into the fleece collar of her jacket.

"Do you live very far away?" I asked.

"No, just a couple of blocks. I used to walk home, back when I was new here. Until the night when I saw one of... Them." She gestured toward the nearby tombstones. "Walking through the graveyard. No, not walking—*floating.* This dark figure. It was tall, much taller than any man. I saw it floating across. That was too much. Since then, I always get a ride home."

I walked up the wooden staircase to my room. A friend's text message buzzed into my phone. *It's almost midnight, David. Are you still doing it?*

Just let me post one last video, I replied.

Luckily, the motel's WiFi was working, and I was able to broadcast a live video from my room. I sat back in the creaky chair and stared at the yellow curtains.

Maggie is from this town, I thought, *and she won't even walk past the graveyard at night. I'm about to walk* into *it.*

I hit the *record* button and spoke into the camera of my laptop.

"When I committed to doing this, I thought I would be connected to you all the whole time. Turns out, I can't broadcast live from my phone. I'm going to have to record a video in the graveyard. Then I'll upload it tomorrow. Assuming I survive."

A few "surprised face" emoticons floated across the screen in response.

I recapped all the stories I had heard about the graveyard from motel employees, guests, and town residents. "I get the impression that if you live here long enough, you're bound to see something you can't explain. And all the stories, all the phenomena, point back to the cemetery."

I kept talking. After five minutes, I realized that I was repeating myself. I hemmed and hawed, dragging it out for as long as I could. I longed to remain connected to the outside world.

"Shit, man," I said to the camera. "It just hit me. I'm really about to go out there."

As soon as I stopped recording, I would be alone. I realized that if I put it off any longer, I would talk myself out of it. I stood to zip up my jacket and put my hat on.

"I'll upload the video after I get back," I said to the computer screen at last. "If I survive."

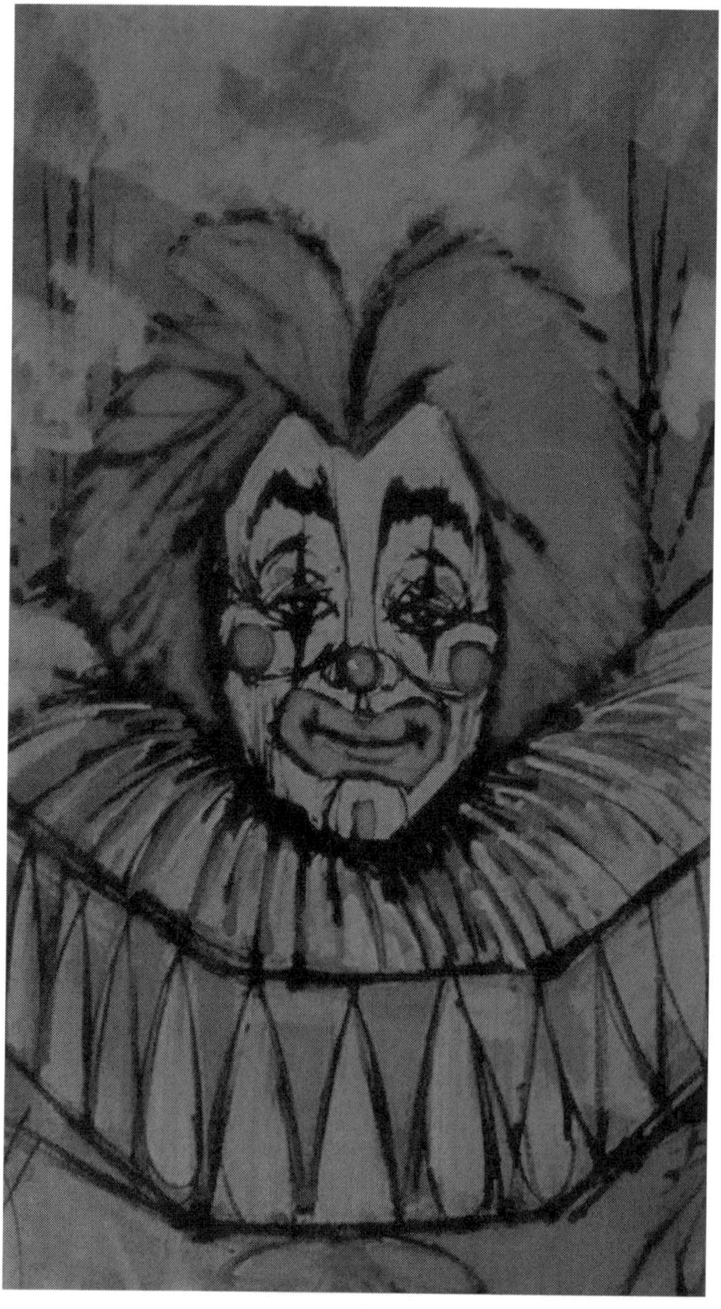

CHAPTER 20

Cemetery

Something called to her that Sunday afternoon, perhaps,
that she could not name.
You and I cannot name it, drawn to each other
by this news.
The young cry when they feel it
breathing beside them.
We may know it sometimes through its disguises,
say, the sound of a car at two a.m.
grinding to a stop in a gravel drive.

    -Jo McDougall, *Upon Hearing About the Suicide of the Daughter of Friends*

I stepped outside and locked my room. The plywood clown on my door stared at me with blank eyes. As I creaked down the faded blue Astroturf of the staircase, my steps fell slowly and deliberately, like a man on his way to the firing squad.

I realized that I would have to move slowly, to allow my phone's camera to focus. This meant I would have to walk slowly through the graveyard as well.

The beam of my flashlight danced across the greasy gravel of the parking lot, casting a spectral blue light. Three cement steps led me to the wrought iron gate of the cemetery. It glowed white against the black sky, the curly design atop the lintel resembling two horns. I recalled the gates of Hell in Dante's *Inferno: Abandon hope, all ye who enter here.*

A wooden grave marker bearing the single name "Charles" glowed in the beam of my flashlight. I stood at the edge of the graveyard. This was it—the thin line dividing the world of the living from the dead. Hades, Xibalbá, the Other Side.

This was where the diner waitress's teenage niece brought her tape recorder and picked up a growling voice. This was where the *Ghost Adventures* crew couldn't get their equipment to work, like "something" didn't want them in here. This was where Maggie saw the dark figure floating past, "much taller than any man." It was where Jack saw lights hovering above the tombstones.

I stared at them and thought I saw a faint light at the far end of the cemetery. *Is that the reflection from a streetlight? A candle someone left on a grave? Or…*

I remembered Brandi's story of the girl who took "orb" photos in the graveyard. She later said that "something" followed her home. As I stood there at the gateway, I had no doubts in my mind—I *knew* there was something out there. Behind every tombstone, that twisted white face I saw at Disneyland was hiding, waiting. Two black holes where its eyes should have been, a clownish grimace on its mouth.

An ancient fear from deep in my chest crept up my spine and spread its fingers across my skull. Every moment of dread in my life flooded my memory.

Walking to school the first day of Junior High, hiding behind my shaggy hair, hoping the bullies wouldn't notice me. Standing in line to board the bus to Sixth Grade Camp. The first day of grade school, my parents out of sight, so far away.

Every nameless, faceless demon and monster lay before me in the dark, behind those tombstones. This was *Me Ixpakinté,* the spirit from southern Mexico who feeds off fear. This was the shape-shifting monster from *IT.* They were real.

I lowered the phone and prayed the Lord's Prayer. My voice shook. When I finished, I pushed a strand of hair from my face and walked forward.

The gravel crunched under my feet. I walked with careful, deliberate steps. My breath came out in short, ragged spurts, like the asthmatic kid in P.E. class. My muscles cramped. Although I was barely moving, I already felt exhausted. It took great effort to hold the phone still. The uncontrollable shaking of my hands had nothing to do with the cold.

The wind froze my eyeballs. Every shape caught in the beam of my flashlight became distorted, otherworldly. I had to blink back tears to see straight.

Most of the grave sites were barebones: a single row of stones marking the outline, a wooden marker at the head. The markers were all shapes and sizes—thin, squat, wide, tall, as varied as the hundreds of clown dolls in the lobby. Beneath each one of them, a rotting human body.

I stared down at the ground as I walked. When the beam of my flashlight hit a wooden grave marker, a great, black shadow stretched behind it, longer and longer. I knew that something horrible waited in that shadow. My light would hit it, and that something would smile back at me with perverse glee. I was sure it was back there.

After I had passed several graves, I looked up to see how far in I was. I hadn't made any progress at all. The dark expanse of the graveyard still loomed ahead of me, as vast and fathomless as when I arrived. The laws of time and space no longer applied.

The freezing, unforgiving wind stung my face. I had never before realized how ghostly the wind sounds when there is no other ambient noise. No cars, no people. Not even a tree for the wind to blow through, rustling its leaves with a calming flutter. In the void of the empty desert cemetery, the wind took on a life of its own. It was an entity with an independent existence, a cold, soulless intelligence that couldn't care whether I lived or died. It snaked and slid between the tombstones, moaning and rattling over their rough edges, mimicking an ethereal voice.

Hoooo...

Haaa...

What had Maggie said? She heard voices in the Clown Motel. Just out of earshot, when she was alone. Speaking words from another world.

I looked up again and saw that I had reached dead center of the cemetery. I was surrounded by the dead.

A grave with a proper cement headstone stood up ahead, surrounded by a black iron fence. Was the fence there to prevent vandalism? Not likely. I hadn't seen a single graffito since I arrived in Tonopah. To keep out grave robbers? I couldn't imagine anything worth stealing. I took a step closer and my foot sank into the sand. Something cracked underneath. A much more chilling possibility came to mind.

Are some of these graves caving in?

I pictured a vivid scene: I step on a grave, the rotting casket caves in beneath me, and I fall into a pile of bones and dust and rotting flesh. I took extra care to watch where I stepped.

A dog barked somewhere in the distance.

Do people here even tie up their dogs at night?

It yelped again, a tremulous, high pitch.

Is that even a dog?

I imagined some coyote or wolf roaming the desert, occasionally wandering into the graveyard to feast on the corpses. Slowly developing a taste for human flesh. I walked more briskly.

The light at the far end of the graveyard glowed brighter.

It's got to be the reflection from a distant streetlight...

Something rustled in the brush, up ahead, in the darkness.

It's just the wind moving the weeds. It's got to be the wind...

I remembered that my camera was still rolling, and addressed my viewers:

"This was a stupid idea. I really wish I wasn't here right now."

I made a few wisecracks for the camera, joking with my public, trying to imagine some happy, future moment when a living human would see this video.

Even as my sarcastic commentary continued, my terror spiraled out of control. It mutated beyond all recognition. I no longer even knew *what* I was afraid of. Whatever waited for me behind the next tombstone was a creature of Lovecraftian proportions, an unspeakable horror that defied my wildest imagination.

It would have been so much easier if I were afraid of something concrete and knowable. If I had a specific idea in my head of *what* I thought I would see, I could handle it. If I believed, for instance, that a reanimated corpse would reach its hand up through the earth and grab my ankle, that would be manageable. A zombie is something you can see and touch.

Whatever lurked in the graveyard was infinitely worse, utterly unknowable. It was the horror hiding at the bottom of the ocean, waiting for me to swim out past the pier. It was the next attack the bullies at school would come up with, more imaginatively cruel than anything that I could fathom.

Something rustled in the brush, louder this time. Even as I told myself it was the wind, I knew it was a lie. Something much worse was coming, something beyond this material world.

I finally understood the true horror of the clowns.

Clowns were not frightening because of how they looked and sounded. They were frightening because of what they concealed. The smiling face and grotesque features were just a facade, a mask covering the real horror. This was what Nietzsche had meant when he talked about staring into the void.

Another sound came from the dry brush.

Okay, that definitely wasn't the wind. Something is moving back there.

I moved forward more slowly. The light was directly ahead of me now, floating three feet above my head. I froze with my heart in my throat. A pale, undulating form, like a thin sheet of light blue, glowed and rustled.

It was a flag. An American flag flapped in the wind beneath a soft blue light bulb. I laughed with relief. That must have been the noise I kept hearing. Someone had set up this flag pole in the graveyard and installed an automatic light above it. I had been worried about nothing. I laughed again, louder.

I heard the rustling again. Something shook in the dry brush ahead of me, beyond the flagpole.

I tiptoed towards the sound. A black, wrought iron fence surrounding a large tombstone at the back edge of the cemetery. I moved slowly closer. I knew this grave. I had seen it before, I was sure of it. It was identical to the one I saw as a child, in the Haunted Mansion at Disneyland. Menacing spikes topped the ornately fence posts. The granite headstone curved upwards in broad, forming a clownish, exaggerated shape.

I leaned forward against the black fence and held my camera closer. Something moved behind the gravestone.

A rustle, a scurry.

A blur of motion in the darkness. I turned my flashlight on it. Something emerging from the shadows, long and white. Flexing, twisting. Tendrils, fingers, bones. My heartbeat pounded in my ears, drowning out all sound.

It was here. It had finally shown itself. The Thing that had lurked in every nightmare since I was five years old, the Thing that would never show its face, that came within inches of me before I woke in a cold sweat, it was finally materializing before me...

The Thing crawled into the beam of my flashlight. It stared at me. Two tiny, black eyes. It jumped free of the brush and sat and stared.

It was a rabbit.

The animal hopped out from behind the grave and ran past me. I screamed.

That was enough for me. I jogged between the tombstones, not caring how the video would look, breathing heavy, cursing, sweeping the beam of my flashlight ahead of me, running towards the bright lights of the Clown Motel in the distance. I dodged the stone outlines of each grave, because the last thing in the world I needed was to have a grave collapse underneath me and fall headfirst into a pile of human remains. I rushed toward the lights, growling ever brighter, away from the dead, away from the cemetery…

The gateway stood ahead of me. The words from *Ichabod Crane and the Headless Horsemen* echoed in my head:

Once you cross that bridge, my friends
The ghost is through, his power ends

I crossed through the gate, ran across the parking lot and up the stairs, unlocked my room with shaking hands, and shut the door behind me.

The Clown Motel never felt so warm and inviting.

CHAPTER 21
"Something Is Here"

"[Monsters]...are the things hiding in history's dark places..."
-W. Scott Poole, *Monsters in America*

I awoke to a knock at the door. I had forgotten where I was. The graveyard... The tombstones... The howling wind... A white, skeletal hand knocking on the lid of its coffin...

"Mr. Schmidt?" A voice called outside my door.

I opened my eyes.

I was in my room. Sunlight streamed in through the old curtains. I was in the hotel, and it was daytime. I was alive.

I pulled on my pants and staggered to the door. Brandi stood there smiling.

"Sleep well, Mr. Schmidt? Sorry to bother you, but I know you wanted to meet Bob Perchetti, the owner. He's here right now, if you want to catch him."

"Thanks, Brandi. I'll be down in ten minutes."

I showered and stepped outside under a bright, cloudless sky. At some point after I got back from the graveyard, it had rained during the night. The morning wind had dried all but a few puddles. The parking lot and the surrounding desert had a bright, freshly washed look. Even the chipped paint of the motel looked whiter.

Jack stood smoking by his truck, wearing his same denim jacket. "Checking out today?" He asked.

I nodded. "I've had enough clowns for one weekend."

"It was nice meetin' you." He tipped his cap. "Have a safe trip back."

I walked into the lobby with a little spring in my step. Brandi stood next to a man in his sixties, of moderate build, with short, silver hair. His warm smile and full cheeks made me think of a human Cabbage Patch doll.

"Mr. Perchetti?" I asked.

"Please, call me Bob," he said with a twinkle in his eye. "Did you enjoy your stay here?"

"Why clowns?" It wasn't the best way to start an interview; and yet, after three nights in the motel, it was the first thing out of my mouth. I waved my hand around the lobby incredulously and repeated the question. "Why all these clowns?"

Bob chuckled. "Believe me, the intention was never to make this into a creepy place. The original owner, LeRoy David, built it in 1987. Clowns were innocent fun back then. I mean, heck, *Circus Circus* has a clown on their sign, and they were one of the first family-friendly hotels in Vegas. Leroy wanted to build a nice place the kids could enjoy here in Tonopah. We're right between Reno and Vegas, and a lot of tourist traffic comes through here."

Bob had the easy-going air of a true "people person." As we talked, locals came and went, greeting him and the staff by name.

"Plus, LeRoy already had a collection of clowns," he continued. "There were so many of them that he eventually said, 'I've got to either sell these clowns or put them to work.' So he put them to work." Bob waved a hand around the lobby and chuckled.

"What about the graveyard next door?" I asked. "I feel like he might have picked a better location. Like, one not so close to all these dead people."

"There's a simple reason for that," Bob said. "LeRoy chose this spot to honor his father, Clarence David. He died in the big mine fire of 1911, and LeRoy built the motel as a tribute, a memorial to him. No different from someone dedicating a song or a book to a loved one."

"That makes sense," I said.

"Trust me, the thought of creating anything dark or creepy never would have crossed his mind. He was a very sweet, innocent soul. He just wanted this to be a fun place for the kids. And that was long before 'killer clowns' were a big thing in the movies."

"It was also before all these weirdos started dressing up like clowns and scaring people."

"Exactly." Bob shook his head. "Isn't that crazy? I feel like the world's gotten a lot more complicated, lately."

"Still," I said, "I can imagine that some kids aren't thrilled by the clowns here."

"It's true. Some families come in here, and the kids are clutching momma's jacket, hiding behind her. I tell them, 'Don't worry. We've got nothing but nice, friendly clowns. There's no mean, ugly clowns in here.'"

"I guess you don't show them this guy," I said as I patted the cage on the desk with the evil clown in it. Bob laughed.

"That's probably why we keep that one way up here, out of reach."

I nodded towards "Mr. Creepy" in his rocking chair. "What's the story on this one?"

"I had him custom made," Bob said. "I know a man in Boulder City who makes figures out of wax. I showed him an old clown painting and said, 'Can you make a doll like this?' He said, 'Sure.'"

I didn't bother to ask why, if he was having a clown custom-made, he would pick such a terrifying face.

"The hands were very lifelike," I said dryly.

"They're carved from wood. In fact, that's the hand that fell off the clown's lap when they filmed that TV show here, *Ghost Adventures*. Personally, I think they used fishing line or something. I've never seen anything strange happen with that doll."

"Well, if I were a ghost," I said, "that's the first doll I'd decide to haunt."

"Maybe you're right," Bob laughed. "You know, come to think of it, we did have one guest who said it 'haunted' him. He told me he woke up in the middle of the night, and he saw that doll standing in his room. At the foot of his bed. He blinked a couple times, rubbed his eyes, and it was still there. Then it disappeared."

"Yikes." I glanced at Mr. Creepy again. I couldn't be sure, but his head seemed to have tilted slightly towards us. "So Bob, how do you feel about the motel's reputation as a haunted place? As its owner, I mean."

"Hey," he said with a mischievous glance, "I figure, I'm fine with whatever brings in the customers. A lot of people come here looking for that kind of thing. They *want* to be scared. Often, they're exactly the people who *don't* experience anything. But then…" He scratched his chin. "Just the other night, for instance. We had a guest—ordinary guy, not your 'ghost hunter' type—who complained about noises. Like someone stomping around the room above him. But nobody *was* in the room above him."

I lowered my voice—reverently, almost. "That happened to me too. The first night I was here."

"Really? Well, there you go, that's another story for us. You're definitely not the first person to experience something strange here." He shrugged. "Who knows? Maybe there really is something here. I just hope we don't get a bad reputation. I don't want people to think they're going to run into some nut dressed as a clown if they stay here. You saw for yourself—what kind of people did you meet here in Tonopah?"

I thought back on Maggie, Brandi, Jack, the waitresses at the diner, and every other local I'd encountered.

"Normal, friendly country folks," I said at last. "Nothing but the best kind of people."

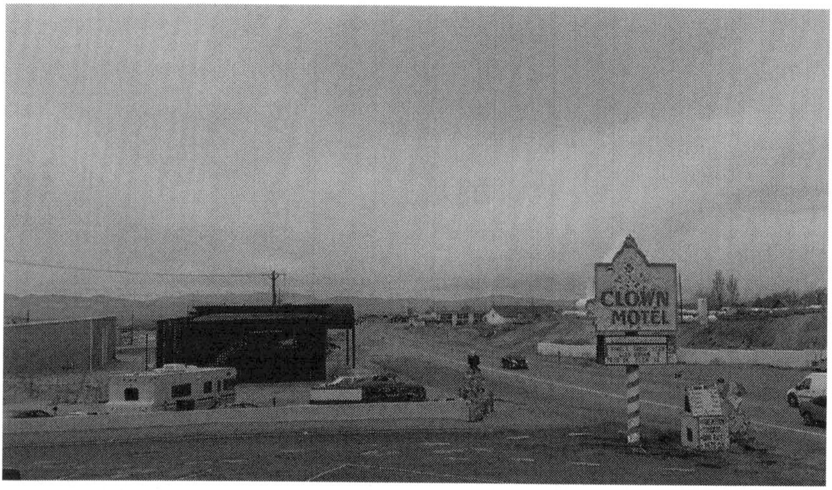
CLOWN
MOTEL

CHAPTER 22

The Clowns I Fear

"...the relationship between fantasy and the horror of the Real it conceals is much more ambiguous than it may seem: fantasy conceals this horror, yet at the same time it creates what it purports to conceal—its 'repressed' point of reference..."
      -Slavoj Zizek, Slovenian philosopher

I thanked Bob for his time and gave him a copy of my book, *Holy Ghosts*. "Hope you enjoy the ghost stories. Maybe you'll find some that are similar to what happens here."

"I look forward to reading it!" He handed me a stack of postcards. "Here, take a few of these for your friends. On the house. Proof that you 'survived' the Clown Motel." He winked. I promised to send him copies of my book about my experience there as well.

When I noticed it was already 12:00 p.m., I asked Brandi if she needed the key right away. "There's no hurry," she said with a smile. "This isn't some big-city hotel where they kick you out right at noon. Take your time."

I packed my things and took one last look around the room. The enormous clown in the painting stared back at me. "Hang in there, big fellah," I said out loud. I half expected him to wink back at me.

Even if he had, I can't imagine it would have frightened me very much. The whole place seemed to have been exorcised of anything menacing. I could have easily spent another week there.

When I went back to the lobby to drop off my key, I gave Bob and Brandi my business cards to stay in touch.

"Oh," Brandi said, "you're a translator!"

"That's my 'day job,' when I'm not writing," I said.

"Do you think you could help us out with something?" Bob pulled a magazine from under the counter. "They wrote this article about our motel a while ago and sent us a copy, but it's all in German."

The magazine *Indie* had a short blurb on the motel. I translated the text out loud, focusing on the positive things the Germans had to say, such as: *Die komfortablen Zimmer haben nur vereinzelt kleine Beldchen von den creepy Spaßvögeln an den Wanden.* (The comfy rooms have only a few small pictures of creepy clowns on the walls.) I didn't bother translating the last line, as it was so eerily on point that it felt incriminating:

Whoever would like to put their fears to the ultimate test can go for a walk through the graveyard adjacent to the motel, and see what happens.

I said goodbye to Brandi and Bob, with firm handshakes and smiles. I was genuinely going to miss them. In the light of day, Tonopah felt like nothing more than a friendly, small town, where everyone was on a first-name basis. In the motel, the diner, the saloon, I had found nothing but hospitality and open arms.

* * * *

The road out of Tonopah carried me serenely across the flat, open countryside. A handful of fluffy white clouds adorned the clear blue sky. I rolled down my window and let the crisp high desert air fill my lungs.

I was alive. I had survived the Clown Motel.

Dozens of horror movies had conditioned me to fear a place like Tonopah. The danger, as the cliché goes, is "out there." *The Hills Have Eyes, The Texas Chainsaw Massacre,* and every cabin-in-the-woods movie ever made. They all hammer the same message home: for civilization and safety, stay in the city. Go out into the country, and you're bound to meet cannibals and undead murderers.

To be sure, Tonopah had a particular *Twin Peaks* mystique about it, a history of strange happenings. Still, I'd be much more worried about the city, when it came to general human insanity.

Life in the city is a double-edged sword. There is protection there, if you can afford it. Your cell phone can help you if you're lost. The police might help you out of a jam. There is a sense of "safety in numbers" that comes with being surrounded by other people.

And yet, modern life is fraught with its own kind of madness.

The city protects you as long as you're an "insider" and can pay the rent; otherwise, it hangs you out to dry. The internet that connects you to the world is also a platform for anonymous bullying. And of course, the city is a place where the violent and the unstable hide in plain sight.

A half hour away from Tonopah, my car radio picked up a fuzzy station broadcasting news about the shooter who held up the bus in Las Vegas. I wish this was one isolated incident, but public shootings have become disturbingly common. Six months after my trip to Nevada, the worst shooting in modern U.S. history took place in the same city.

Many people are frightened by the grotesque imagery of clowns—their exaggerated features, crazy faces, and funny voices. I think there is another reason, though: we fear the human evil that can hide behind the mask. We fear the "shadow," as Carl Jung would say, the dark side of humanity. Humans have done terrible things to each other while hiding behind a mask.

We put a ski mask on to rob each other.

We anonymously harass our peers online.

We put on hoods and sheets and terrorize those who are different.

We often abuse our authority, torturing and raping and murdering when we feel impunity, when we think nobody's watching.

The truly diabolical is not to be found in the exotic image of the killer clown, but in the base, everyday grayness of human cruelty. The real savagery is not out there in the desert—it is all around us.

These are the clowns to fear—whether or not they paint their faces.

* * * *

An hour outside of Tonopah, I stopped in the town of Beatty for breakfast. The casino on the edge of town had a Denny's and a reliable WiFi connection. I ate a sandwich and used the internet to upload my graveyard video. The cold tombstones already felt a million miles away.

While I was online, a message came in from a friend in Mexico City. She knows about my interest in anthropology, and sent me an article about an folk tradition from southern Mexico. It happened to involve clowns.

The Mixtec indigenous community of Santa Rosa, Oaxaca, practice an ancient form of clowning. The town's *Maromeros* paint their faces and perform acrobatics during their annual festival. The clowns of Santa Rosa are a unique mix between the court jesters of medieval Spain and ancient, pre-Hispanic masked dancers. They dance, jump, and laugh. They twirl and dangle from ropes and bars, performing improvised acrobatics.

They delight in the absurd, the inappropriate and burlesque, challenging the boundaries of social propriety. The ancient clown's main purpose was not to make us laugh with mirth or tremble with fear: it was to challenge social norms. *Caminan por el filo entre el bien y el mal,* as the article says—they walk the line between good and evil. In doing so, they bring clowning back to its historic origins.

They mock our self-righteousness. They interrogate the privilege of those in power. This tradition of purpose-driven clowning exists across the globe. It is present in the "trickster" legends of the Native peoples of North America, in the figures of Raven, Coyote and *Kokopelli*.

It is present in the "Holy Fool" of Eastern Orthodoxy, and is a central part of much more ancient forms of Christianity. As far back as the Apostle Paul, theologians have taught "the Law" exists for one sole purpose—to prove that it doesn't work. It is impossible to live a perfect, flawless life. In more simplified language: clowns teach us not to take ourselves too seriously.

These *Maromeros* also confront the dark impulses—sex and aggression—that can be frightening. They mock these human drives. With their gruesome appearance, they mock death itself. They plumb the depths of what we fear, the enemies from within and without, showing us that the darkness will not overcome us. Indeed, it can even be laughed at.

In the ancient traditions of Mexico's indigenous peoples, masks did not exist to hide one's identity for violent purposes. They allowed humans to become supernatural beings, to explore the space between the profane and the sacred. This ancient wisdom is still alive. The native Mixtec name for San Jerónimo Sayucatlán, a village in the State of Puebla, is *Ñuu sa'nu sa'a yuku ña'na*: "the people of the mask."

These festivals keep communities like Santa Rosa intact. Even migrants who have been working in the United States send back money to support the celebration. *Maromeros* are the polar opposite of the antisocial "evil clown." Rather, they are the glue that holds the community together.

This is the original, ancient purpose of the clown. To maintain social cohesion, even while questioning the values we take for granted. Their role is invaluable. Some might even say it is sacred—the holy clown.

THREE NIGHTS IN THE CLOWN MOTEL

CHAPTER 23
A Lovely Day in Death Valley

Kiser [of Ringling Bros. and Barnum & Bailey Circus], of course, doesn't see clowning diminishing in the slightest. But good clowns are always in shortage, and it's good clowns who keep the art alive.

-Linda Rodriguez McRobbie, "The History and Psychology of Clowns Being Scary," *Smithsonian*, published on July 31, 2013.

I finished my breakfast in Beatty and got back on the road. The highway went straight downhill from there, across the Nevada border into Death Valley. It descended in a straight line, cutting the flat panorama neatly in two. I could easily see a hundred miles down the road.

I thought back on my trip up to Tonopah, just three days ago.

In the warm light of day, Death Valley felt picturesque and serene. A perfect, azure sky hung over the desert. The late afternoon sun painted the desert with a warm, soft palette: the tawny color of freshly baked pastry; the burnt yellows of an inviting haystack at an Autumn carnival. The colors of comfort.

Herds of cyclists rode alongside the highway, wearing neon-colored Spandex shorts. This was the sign of ultimate safety—grown men who felt comfortable appearing outside half-naked.

This was where, just three days ago, monsters and demons had lurked around every bend. When I could only see a few yards ahead, the darkness was terrifying. Now that I could see 100 miles down the road, the vast expanses of space were breathtakingly gorgeous. The difference was literally one of night and day.

There was a savage beauty to the desert. Ravines cut up the sides of mountains, like the time-earned wrinkles of an old man's weathered face. Desert brush and chaparral grew on the hillsides. The hellish nightmare had transformed into a majestic matte painting.

Most horror stories are missing this element of redemption. Most end in despair and darkness. To paraphrase Father Merrin from *The Exorcist*: "I think the point is to make us despair. To see ourselves as animal and ugly. To make us reject the possibility that God could love us." When the darkness has been confronted, though, it transforms. The black valley of death becomes beauty incarnate.

I came to a flat expanse of sand, punctuated by jagged, yellow arrow weed shrubs. They looked like mischievous, bushy-haired dwarves crouched by the roadside. A sign informed me that this was "The Devil's Cornfield."

In the daylight, this valley was no longer the haunt of the devils that besot my childhood. Rather, the word recovered the playful meaning of folk sayings: Devil's food cake. "A handsome devil." The Tasmanian devil.

Like the original Greek meaning of the term "daemon," these "devils" were the wild, untamed spirits of nature. As such, they were the opposite of anything truly diabolical—they were the savage, wild beautify in which the majesty of Creation is most clearly seen.

As I drove through Death Valley, I felt absolute peace. I could drive down that road all day long.

* * * *

The Devil's Cornfield was followed by the sand dunes of the lowlands. They stretched for miles into the distance, like a Hollywood depiction of the Sahara Desert. I parked at a rest stop and got out to stretch my legs.

The warm, dry air was a refreshing change from the icy chill of the high desert. A flock of cars and RVs by the dunes suggested the abundance of families who hiked, frolicked, and leisurely explored them. I parked and joined the families of all nationalities who came to escape the anxiety of the city.

Pure, spotless sand stretched to the horizon. In this tranquil place where nothing grew, nothing needed to grow. Desert and jungle, light and dark, sand and vegetation, they are all part of the same living, breathing planet that sustains us.

A three year old boy crouched behind a bush. He covered his face with a blanket and jumped out at his parents with a fierce growl. "Ah, scary!" they cried melodramatically. The boy laughed, reveling in the chance to become someone else behind the mask.

Elderly retired couples stood sipping sodas in the shadows of their mobile homes. One pale, Russian family sat on the rocks eating a picnic of black bread and slices of salami. A couple of blonde German nymphs in flowing white dresses took photos of each other, jumping in the air off the dunes, laughing white teeth smiles, exposing long, tan legs. Children rolled down the dunes in clouds of sand, giggling and shouting.

I got back on the road and came to a long, solitary stretch of highway, with no people or cyclists. I played my old CD collection with the windows down, singing along to songs I hadn't heard for ten years. The warm wind caressed my face. The rugged beauty of the desert invigorated me.

Then I saw him.

Wait... Is that...?

His bright costume swelled about his form in a flash of red and yellows, billowing in the wind.

No, it can't be...

A flash of color, a face. Standing by the roadside, looking straight at me.

No, it is... It's a clown.

He stood with both hands to his face, smearing white paint across his cheeks, elbows akimbo. Black, gaping holes where his eyes should have been. I slowed down and stared.

He was a tourist.

His car stood parked in the sand by the roadside. His baggy, Hawaiian shirt blew in the wind, the red and yellow flowers undulating. Probably a European, judging by the black socks he wore with his sandals. He slathered sunscreen on his pasty skin, his eyes hidden behind large, round sunglasses.

He waved at me. I waved back, wiped the sweat from my brow, and drove the rest of the way home.

-David J. Schmidt, 2017

THREE NIGHTS IN THE CLOWN MOTEL

FOR MORE INFORMATION

You can see all my videos from the Clown Motel at the links below. If you're interested in other haunted places, check out my book *Holy Ghosts: True Tales from a Haunted Christian College*, which goes into several theories about ghosts and hauntings.
https://www.amazon.com/Holy-Ghosts-Haunted-Christian-College/dp/1511704675

You can also check out my website. You'll get the first book in my *Tiny Staircase* series, about ghosts and strange phenomena, for free. Enjoy!
www.HolyGhostStories.com

Clown Motel videos
Inside the lobby of the Clown Motel (Chapter 7)
https://www.youtube.com/watch?v=OcCZX5B0A0s

Lobby video in Spanish (Chapter 7)
https://www.youtube.com/watch?v=JqbItp-P7gs

"Confessional" video describing the terrors of the first night (Chapter 9)
https://www.youtube.com/watch?v=jPrBDExMhCY

Video taken live during the second night, investigating strange noises (Chapter 13)
https://www.youtube.com/watch?v=1Y5SYDlidQM

Midnight walk through the cemetery (Chapter 19)
https://www.youtube.com/watch?v=B2xpkkxwnyk

Sources Cited

King, Stephen. *IT.* New York, Viking: 1986.

Introduction
Andrew Stott quoted in:
Linda Rodriguez McRobbie, "The History and Psychology of Clowns Being Scary," *Smithsonian,* published July 31, 2013.
http://www.smithsonianmag.com/arts-culture/the-history-and-psychology-of-clowns-being-scary-20394516/

Vox poll on clown fear:
http://www.vox.com/2016/10/21/13321536/clown-scare-sightings-2016

Sources of international news about clown sightings:
Australia:
http://www.adelaidenow.com.au/news/south-australia/creepy-clown-terrorises-two-12yearold-girls-in-adelaides-cbd/news-story/54185eba7682d55a5259a9f10241c88d

Finland:
http://www.hs.fi/kotimaa/a1476760926838

Ireland:
http://www.irishmirror.ie/news/irish-news/young-girl-terrified-after-creepy-9036686

Chapter 1
Deep Thoughts by Jack Handey
https://www.deepthoughtsbyjackhandey.com/

News on suicide jumpers in San Diego:
http://www.sandiegouniontribune.com/news/public-safety/sd-me-freeway-jumper-20170331-story.html

Steinbeck, John. *Travels with Charley in Search of America.* New York: Penguin Books, 1980.

Chapter 2
Tony Merevick, "Clown porn searches have skyrocketed thanks to the creepy clown epidemic," *Thrill List*, published October 14, 2016.
https://www.thrillist.com/news/nation/creepy-clown-epidemic-clown-porn-searches-are-way-up-according-to-pornhub.

Article on Chris Sebela's month spent in the Clown Motel:
http://kernelmag.dailydot.com/issue-sections/features-issue-sections/16554/haunted-clown-motel-christopher-sebela-kickstarter/

Chapter 3
Katie Rogers, "Creepy clown sightings in South Carolina Cause a Frenzy," *New York Times,* published August 31, 2016.
https://www.nytimes.com/2016/08/31/us/creepy-clown-sightings-in-south-carolina-cause-a-frenzy.html?_r=1

Chapter 4
Edmond de Goncourt quoted in:
Linda Rodriguez McRobbie, "The History and Psychology of Clowns Being Scary," *Smithsonian,* published on July 31, 2013.
http://www.smithsonianmag.com/arts-culture/the-history-and-psychology-of-clowns-being-scary-20394516/

John Wayne Gacy quoted in:

Sullivan, Terry and Maiken, Peter T. *Killer Clown: The John Wayne Gacy Murders.* New York: Pinnacle Books, Windsor Publishing Corp., 1983.

Chapter 5
Twin Peaks. Episode #2.11. Directed by Duwayne Dunham. Written by Mark Frost, David Lynch, and Barry Pullman. ABC, December 15 1990.

Chapter 6
The Simpsons. "Lisa's First Word." Season 4, Episode 10. Directed by Mark Kirkland. Written by Matt Groening, James L. Brooks, Sam Simon, and Jeff Martin. FOX, December 3, 1992.

Chapter 7
Dickens, Charles. *The Pickwick Papers (Wordsworth Classics).* New York: Wordsworth Classics, 1992.

Chapter 8
David Caplan, "Police Arrest Woman in 'Killer Clown' Cold Case," *Good Morning America,* published September 27, 2017. https://www.yahoo.com/gma/police-arrest-woman-killer-clown-cold-case-054905739--abc-news-topstories.html

Chapter 9
Dr. Penny Curtis quoted in:
"Hospital Clown Images Too Scary," *BBC News,* last updated Tuesday, January 15, 2008, http://news.bbc.co.uk/2/hi/health/7189401.stm

Creepy clown videos and news:
http://vancouversun.com/news/local-news/creepy-clown-prank-spreads-to-b-c

CREEPY CLOWN SIGHTING CAUGHT ON CAMERA - QUEBEC CANADA 2016
https://www.youtube.com/watch?v=jNV8cfexzX4
Uploaded October 3, 2016

1986 Disneyland Circus Fantasy Commercial
https://www.youtube.com/watch?v=RB4xOYnrDw0
Uploaded May 15, 2016

Chapter 10
Seinfeld. "The Opera," Episode 9, Season 4. Directed by Tom Cherones. Written by Larry David and Jerry Seinfeld. NBC, November 4 1992.

Chapter 11
"Victim recognizes teen during brutal attack by 20 people in 'The Purge,' clown masks," *WFTV9 ABC*, last updated November 1, 2016.
http://www.wftv.com/news/local/victim-recognizes-teen-during-brutal-attack-by-20-people-in-the-purge-clown-masks/462664786

Devereux, Paul. *Haunted Land: Investigations into Ancient Mysteries and Modern Day Phenomena.* London: Judy Piatkus Publishers Limited, 2001.

Rosemary's Baby. Directed by Roman Polanski. Los Angeles: Paramount Pictures, 1968.

Chapter 12
Andrew McConnell Stott quoted in:
Linda Rodriguez McRobbie, "The History and Psychology of Clowns Being Scary," *Smithsonian,* published July 31, 2013.

http://www.smithsonianmag.com/arts-culture/the-history-and-psychology-of-clowns-being-scary-20394516/

Chapter 13
"Police investigating report of a woman attacked by man in clown mask in Winchester, Kentucky," *WDRB News,* published October 1, 2016.
http://www.wdrb.com/story/33293981/police-woman-attacked-by-man-in-clown-mask-in-winchester-ky

Chapter 14
Patricia Doorbar quoted in:
"Hospital Clown Images Too Scary," *BBC News,* last updated Tuesday, January 15, 2008, http://news.bbc.co.uk/2/hi/health/7189401.stm

Chapter 15
T.J. Parker, Rose-Ann Aragon, "Clown attack forces several schools in Ohio to cancel Friday's classes," *WCPO,* published September 29, 2016.
http://www.abc15.com/news/national/creepy-clown-sightings-increase-across-greater-cincinnati

Chapter 16
Andrew Scott, "Cresco men guilty in Juggalo murder trial," *Pocono Record,* published September 22, 2011.
http://www.poconorecord.com/article/20110922/NEWS/109220309

Chapter 18
Huw Silk, "Clowns 'running through gardens and peering through windows' according to police," *Wales Online,* last updated October 10, 2016.

http://www.walesonline.co.uk/news/wales-news/clowns-running-through-gardens-peering-12004301

Chapter 19
Lewis, C.S. *That Hideous Strength.* New York: Collier Books, 1965.

Chapter 20
Jo McDougall, *Upon Hearing About the Suicide of the Daughter of Friends*, 1991.
http://poetryschmmapoetry.blogspot.com/2010/11/upon-hearing-about-suicide-of-daughter.html

Chapter 21
Poole, W. Scott. *Monsters in America. Our Historical Obsession with the Hideous and the Haunting.* Waco: Baylor University Press, 2014.

Chapter 22
Zizek, Slavoy. *The Plague of Fantasies (The Essential Zizek).* Second edition. London: Verso, 2009.

Chapter 23
Linda Rodriguez McRobbie, "The History and Psychology of Clowns Being Scary," *Smithsonian,* published on July 31, 2013.
http://www.smithsonianmag.com/arts-culture/the-history-and-psychology-of-clowns-being-scary-20394516/

The Exorcist. Directed by William Friedkin. Los Angeles: Warner Bros., 1973.

THREE NIGHTS IN THE CLOWN MOTEL

About the author

David J. Schmidt is an author, multilingual translator, home brewer, and professional storyteller. He splits his time between Mexico City and San Diego, CA.

Schmidt has published a variety of books, short stories, and articles in English and Spanish. His English-language titles include ***Holy Ghosts: True Tales from a Haunted Christian College***, a study of haunted places, as well as the series ***Into the Serpent's Head***, regarding his journeys to the remote mountains of Oaxaca, Mexico.

His books published in Mexico include ***Más frío que la nieve: cuentos sobrenaturales de Rusia*** and ***Tunguska: luces en el cielo sobre Siberia***.

Schmidt speaks ten languages and has been to 30 countries. He received his B.A. in Psychology from Point Loma Nazarene University.

THREE NIGHTS IN THE CLOWN MOTEL

Website: www.holyghoststories.com
Facebook: @HolyGhostStories
Twitter: @SchmidtTales
Email: HolyGhostStories@gmail.com

Made in the USA
Columbia, SC
29 July 2023